Heroes and Villains

Louis Pasteur

Louis Pasteur

Other books in the Heroes and Villains series include:

Heroes and Villains

Louis Pasteur

Elizabeth Silverthorne

LUCENT
BOOKS®

THOMSON

™

GALE

San Diego • Detroit • New York • San Francisco • Cleveland • New Haven. Conn. • Waterville. Maine • London • Munich

For more information, contact
Lucent Books
27500 Drake Rd.
Farmington Hills, MI 48331-3535
Or you can visit our Internet site at http://www.gale.com

LIBRARY OF CONGRESS CATALOGING-IN-PUBLICATION DATA

Silverthorne, Elizabeth.
  Louis Pasteur / Elizabeth Silverthorne.
    v. cm. — (Heroes and villains series)
Includes bibliographical references and index.
Summary: Discusses the life of Louis Pasteur and his contributions to fighting disease, creating vaccines, and researching the pasteurization process.
  ISBN 1-59018-308-8
  1. Pasteur, Louis, 1822–1895—Juvenile literature. 2. Scientists—France—Biography— Juvenile literature. 3. Microbiologists—France—Biography—Juvenile literature.
I. Title. II. Series.
  Q143.P2S48 2004
  579'.092—dc22
                                                          2004006306

Contents

Foreword

Good and evil are an ever-present feature of human history. Their presence is reflected through the ages in tales of great heroism and extraordinary villainy. Such tales provide insight into human nature, whether they involve two people or two thousand, for the essence of heroism and villainy is found in deeds rather than in numbers. It is the deeds that pique our interest and lead us to wonder what prompts a man or woman to perform such acts.

Samuel Johnson, the eminent eighteenth-century English writer, once wrote, "The two great movers of the human mind are the desire for good, and fear of evil." The pairing of desire and fear, possibly two of the strongest human emotions, helps explain the intense fascination people have with all things good and evil—and, by extension, heroic and villainous.

People are attracted to the person who reaches into a raging river to pull a child from what could have been a watery grave for both, and to the person who risks his or her own life to shepherd hundreds of desperate black slaves to safety on the Underground Railroad. We wonder what qualities these heroes possess that enable them to act against self-interest, and even their own survival. We also wonder if, under similar circumstances, we would behave as they do.

Evil, on the other hand, horrifies as well as intrigues us. Few people can look upon the drifter who mutilates and kills a neighbor or the dictator who presides over the torture and murder of thousands of his own citizens without feeling a sense of revulsion. And yet, as Joseph Conrad writes, we experience "the fascination of the abomination." How else to explain the overwhelming success of a book such as Truman Capote's *In Cold Blood*, which examines in horrifying detail a vicious and senseless murder that took place in the American heartland in the 1960s? The popularity of murder mysteries and Court TV are also evidence of the human fascination with villainy.

Most people recoil in the face of such evil. Yet most feel a deep-seated curiosity about the kind of person who could commit a terrible act. It is perhaps a reflection of our innermost fears that we wonder whether we could resist or stand up to such behavior in our presence or even if we ourselves possess the capacity to commit such terrible crimes.

The Lucent Books Heroes and Villains series capitalizes on our fascination with the perpetrators of both good and evil by introducing readers to some of history's most revered heroes and hated villains. These include heroes such as Frederick Douglass, who knew firsthand the humiliation of slavery and, at great risk to himself, publicly fought to abolish the institution of slavery in America. It also includes villains such as Adolf Hitler, who is remembered both for the devastation of Europe and for the murder of 6 million Jews and thousands of Gypsies, Slavs, and others whom Hitler deemed unworthy of life.

Each book in the Heroes and Villains series examines the life story of a hero or villain from history. Generous use of primary and secondary source quotations gives readers eyewitness views of the life and times of each individual as well as enlivens the narrative. Notes and annotated bibliographies provide stepping-stones to further research.

An Awesome Career

Louis Pasteur's scientific accomplishments have made his name known throughout the world. Working in primitive laboratories with crude equipment, Pasteur made discoveries in chemistry, microbiology, and medicine that not only revolutionized scientific thinking but changed the way people lived. His intuitive genius and tremendous capacity for work, his diligent research to find answers to questions, his boldness in taking risks, and even his tremendous ambition resulted in a career that is awesome to contemplate. It is truly astounding that one man could achieve so many different goals in one lifetime.

Émile Duclaux, Pasteur's friend and collaborator, wrote,

A mind of a scientific man is a bird on the wing; we see it only when it alights or when it takes flight. We may by watching closely keep it in view, and point out just where it touches the earth. But why does it alight here and not there? Why has it taken this direction and not that in its flight toward new discoveries?[1]

When asked why his career had taken so many different directions, Pasteur's reply was that he considered his work to be the result of a logical progression. He believed that one important discovery led to another important discovery and that each discovery represented a link in an unbroken chain. For example, Pasteur's discovery while working with crystals that organic molecules are not symmetrical opened his mind to insights that helped him as he began his studies on alcoholic fermentation.

Pasteur's work on fermentation, in turn, led him to conduct experiments to prove that the dust in the air carries germs that cause decay and putrefaction. This discovery led to Pasteur's vigorous advo- cacy of the germ theory of disease, which led to his campaign for the practice of antiseptic medicine and surgery and ulti- mately the saving of countless lives. It also led to the process that became known as

Louis Pasteur made significant contributions to the fields of medicine, chemistry, and microbiology that revolutionized scientific thinking and radically improved the quality of life.

A researcher works with an experimental cancer vaccine at the Pasteur Institute in Paris, where researchers continue to investigate ways to cure and prevent disease.

pasteurization, which helped the ailing wine industry in France and taught food and beverage producers how to treat their products so that they would resist spoiling. In addition, Pasteur's insights into the world of bacteria and viruses led to the development of vaccines to prevent diseases in animals, such as cholera in chickens, anthrax in sheep and cattle, and erysipelas in swine.

The final, most famous link in Pasteur's chain of research was the development of a vaccine against rabies in humans. This discovery resulted in the establishment of a research institute in Paris, which was dubbed the "Rabies Palace" by the media of the day. From its beginning, the Pasteur Institute grew into an international network of research facilities. In these laboratories the work of finding ways to prevent and cure diseases continues today, more than 115 years after the institute's founding.

In his speech at the opening of the Paris institute, Pasteur spoke these words, which are as true in the twenty-first century as they were in 1888:

> Two contrary laws seem to be wrestling with each other nowadays; the one, a law of blood and of death, ever imagining new means of destruction and forcing nations to be constantly ready for the battlefield—the other, a law of peace, work and health, ever evolving new means of delivering man from the scourges which beset him.[2]

As much as it was possible for one man in one brief lifetime, Louis Pasteur did all that he could to deliver humanity from some of the worst scourges ever known.

Chapter One

A Very Serious Young Person

No one observing Louis Pasteur during his early years could have predicted that the quiet little boy would grow up to be a living legend. There were, however, influences at work shaping his character and ingraining values in him that would guide him all of his life. Among the most important influences was his family, especially his father, Jean-Joseph, who instilled in his young son a fierce patriotism and an admiration for men who accomplished great things for France's glory. In addition, as Louis watched his father toiling at his difficult trade, he learned the value of patience and perseverance in achieving success.

The Family

Just two days after Christmas, on December 27, 1822, Louis Pasteur was born in a small room in the home of his parents, Jean-Joseph and Jeanne Pasteur. The other member of the family was Virginie, who was four years old at the time. Louis was followed by two more sisters, Josephine in 1825 and Emilie in 1826.

The Pasteurs' home was located above Jean-Joseph's tannery in the town of Dole, on the eastern edge of France. But before Louis was five, the family would move two times as Jean-Joseph sought out a better location for his business. First, they went to Marnoz, where they lived with Jeanne Pasteur's mother. However, Jean-Joseph did not do well in the tanning business there. Then in 1827 they moved to the neighboring town of Arbois, a wine-producing town at the foot of the Jura Mountains.

The family of six moved into a stone house on the banks of the Cuisance River that had already been outfitted as a tannery by a previous tenant. The courtyard in back of the house was filled with seven round pits lined with oakwood for soaking raw animal skins. An outside stairway led down to the tannery in the basement, where the hides received further treatment. On the ground floor were the pantry and laundry room, two bedrooms, and a large kitchen with a window looking out over the river. It was here that the family took their meals. On the upper floor were more bedrooms and the curriery, where the prepared

Significant Places in Pasteur's Life

ENGLAND

GERMANY

FRANCE

SPAIN

Bay of Biscay

Mediterranean Sea

Lille •

Paris ⊛
• Pouilly le Fort

Strasbourg •

Besançon •
Dole • •
Arbois

Clermont-Ferrand •

Bordeaux

Ales •

Marseilles

leather was dressed by scraping, beating, cleansing, and coloring.

As soon as Louis was able to understand his stories, Jean-Joseph told his son of his exciting career as a soldier in the army of Napoleon Bonaparte. In his early twenties Jean-Joseph had fought in Napoleon's bloody Spanish campaign and had been made a chevalier (knight) of the Legion of Honor. Jean-Joseph hung a portrait of Napoleon on the wall of the tannery, and on Sundays he wore his red Legion of Honor ribbon. Louis soon came to realize that following Napoleon as he attempted

Pasteur's father Jean-Joseph owned a successful tannery (where raw hides are made into leather) in a small village in eastern France.

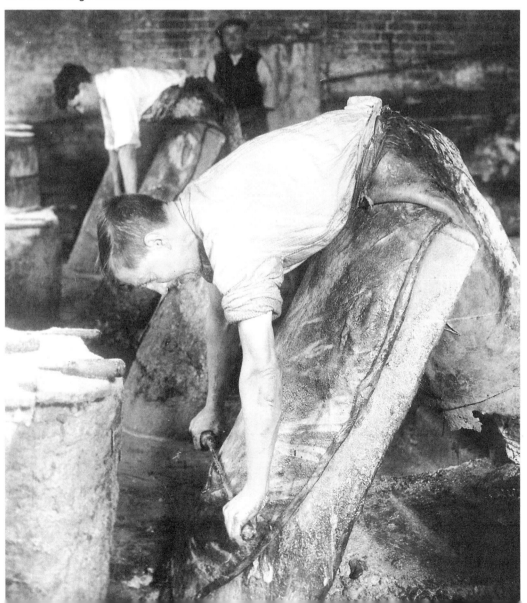

The Sword of Honor

Pasteur's fervent nationalism was instilled in him by his father at an early age. Over the parlor mantel in the home where Louis Pasteur grew up hung a sword that represented a time when Jean-Joseph had been more than a humble tanner working at a dirty, tedious job. As soon as the Pasteur children were old enough to understand, their father told them the story of the sword and passed on to them his own passionate love of France and regret for the passing of the glorious days when Napoleon Bonaparte was a conquering hero and Jean-Joseph had fought in his army. Napoleon himself had awarded the Sword of Honor to Jean-Joseph for bravery in battle. When Napoleon was overthrown, his former officers were ordered to surrender their sabers, but Jean-Joseph could not bear to surrender the sword with which he had fought for his country. He sprang on the agent holding it and wrested it away from him. A sympathetic officer understood his feelings and Jean-Joseph was permitted to keep the sword.

to make France a glorious empire had been the most important time of his father's life. Jean-Joseph's work as a tanner, Louis understood, was just a means of providing a living.

Providing that living was hard work, but as they grew older, the children were able to help with some of the easier tasks connected with the tannery. Jean-Joseph, however, made it clear that he did not want his son to follow the family trade. He hoped that Louis would become a teacher, for teachers were greatly respected in small provincial towns like Arbois.

Early Impressions

Louis was a serious, quiet boy, but he liked playing with friends (many of them the children of the vintners, or winemakers) who lived in the area. In their games in the tannery yard they used stray bits of bark and pieces of iron that were lying about. Sometimes there were scraps of soft leather that could be made into slingshots. They also played marbles and ball games. In the winter Louis and his friends slid on the ice on wooden shoes or in sleds; in summer they swam or fished in the Cuisance. When they were small, the fishing was done from the bridge over the river, but as they grew older they were allowed to go upstream to spearfish for trout.

In school, Louis attracted notice from his teachers with his talent for drawing and painting. He often copied the engravings in his schoolbooks using charcoal or pencil. Louis's teachers encouraged him in this art, as did his mother, who gave him a set of colored drawing pencils.

The Pasteur children enjoyed the life of their village. Everybody knew everybody else in Arbois, and children wandered freely up and down the main street, watching the boot maker or the blacksmith at work or stopping at the livery stable to look at the horses. Louis's favorite shop was the pharmacy. He would stand there quietly by the marble worktable watching intently as the pharmacist ground dried plants into powder and mixed different colored liquids together. He also enjoyed listening to the pharmacist's customers who sought medicines to alleviate their aches and pains or something to cure their sick animals.

During a visit to the blacksmith at the age of eight, Louis saw something that he never forgot. A rabid wolf had come down from the foothills of the Jura Mountains, attacking and biting humans and animals in its path. A bite from a rabid animal was serious, since the victim could develop rabies, a fatal disease for which there was no cure. Some of the victims were taken to the blacksmith's shop to be treated by the only known remedy at that time, which was to have a red-hot iron applied to the wounds to cauterize them. The cauterization was done both to stop bleeding and in an attempt to prevent the victim from developing the disease. This crude treatment, which did not always keep the victim from developing rabies, caused agonizing pain. The terrible scene and the screams of the victims were horrifying.

Schooling in Arbois

Louis attended elementary school, which in Arbois was held in spare rooms of the town hall. Grades one through three met in the same room, and the busy teacher chose dependable third graders as monitors to help teach first graders. Being a monitor was considered an honor, and Louis worked hard until he became one. Despite his dedication, he was such a deliberate and cautious worker that the teacher considered him only an average student.

Louis was not only deliberate but ambitious as well, and when he began attending the College d'Arbois (equivalent to an American high school today), he worked hard to improve his standing as a student. That effort paid off. In his last term at the school (1837–1838) he did so well that the principal recommended to Jean-Joseph that his son be sent to study at the École Normale Supérieure in Paris, a teacher training school where the best students in France were made into elite teachers. Eager to further Louis's prospects, Jean-Joseph sent Louis to a private boarding school in Paris that prepared students for admission to the École Normale.

First Paris Trip

Louis's good friend Jules Vercel was also going to the preparatory school, so on a bitterly cold day in late October 1838 they left their little village, huddled together under a tarpaulin behind the coachman, headed for one of the busiest cities in the world. Fifteen-year-old Louis had never been away from his family before, and he had a hard time adjusting to his new life. Although the teachers at the school were kind and helpful, Louis hated having to wear a uniform and being summoned to class by a drumroll. Above all, he was homesick. "If I could only catch a whiff of the tannery," he told Jules, "I would feel better."[3]

The headmaster of the school became concerned as he watched his young charge sink into a brooding melancholy that grew deeper with every passing day. Louis had always been quiet, but as he became increasingly withdrawn, the headmaster decided to write to Louis's parents about his symptoms. As a result, one day in mid-November Louis was summoned from class to meet a visitor who was waiting for him in a small café. That visitor turned out to be his father, who had come to take him home—less than a month after he had left.

A Talent for Drawing

Louis was relieved to be back with his family in Arbois, but he was upset with himself for letting his feelings rob him of the opportunity he had been offered. For

A nineteenth-century drawing depicts a rabid wolf attacking a group of picnickers. As a child, Pasteur observed as the local blacksmith cauterized the wounds of victims of a similar attack.

solace, he turned to art. As a young boy Louis had become proficient in the technique of portrait painting using pastels. Now he began to employ his talent, which was far beyond the ordinary. Louis used his family and friends and local people in Arbois as his models. He was interested in portraying people realistically, and he observed his subjects closely. His portraits showed great detail, including wrinkles and frowns and usually serious expressions. His portrait of his mother captured her pale blue eyes, pinched lips, and white bonnet tied under her chin with brown curls showing. He depicted his father dressed in a coat with wide lapels and with a wrinkled brow. He also portrayed a barrel maker, the mayor of Arbois, a nun with a pleated headdress, and a local official's big, red face with great precision.

In those days, before the invention of photography, it is possible that Louis Pasteur could have made a living as a portrait painter, as some of his teachers suggested. Louis's father, however, had other ambitions for his son. His heart was still set on sending Louis to Paris to study to become a teacher. This time, however, he would not send him so far away from home for his preparatory training.

Studies at Besançon

It was decided that Louis would prepare himself for the École Normale at a school in Besançon, a nearby city where Jean-Joseph went six times a year to sell his goods. Besançon, only twenty-five miles from Arbois, had a good preparatory school, the College Royal de Franche-Comte, where Louis enrolled as a student in phi-

Pasteur's Tribute to His Parents

After he was grown, many people thought of Louis Pasteur as an unemotional, hardworking scientist, but Pasteur could be very emotional and even sentimental where his family was concerned. In Louis Pasteur and the Hidden World of Microbes, *Louise E. Robbins quotes Pasteur's tribute to his parents given at an 1883 ceremony in which a historical plaque was dedicated at Pasteur's birthplace in Dole.*

Oh! my father and my mother! Oh! my dear departed ones, who lived so modestly in this little house, I owe everything to you! . . . You, my dear father, whose life was as harsh as your harsh trade, you showed me what can be done with patience for sustained effort. It is to you that I owe my tenacity in daily work. Not only did you have the quality of perseverance that makes people's lives useful, but you also had admiration for great men and great things.

losophy. At first his quiet manner and inclination to withdraw inside himself made it difficult for Louis to form friendships with the other students and the teachers. However, he eventually discovered that by drawing portraits he could please people and make friends with them. His first portrait was of the headmaster of the school, who liked it so much he hung it in his front parlor. The next pastel was of the son of the vice principal, who hung it in his office. Louis then went on to delight his classmates by drawing portraits of them in their blue uniforms with gold buttons.

During this time Louis developed a close friendship with Charles Chappuis, the son of a notary (an official who authenticates and records legal documents). The two studied together and spent their leisure time together and came to respect each other for their abilities and talents. More than simply respecting his friend, Louis relied on him for emotional support. If Louis was in one of his taciturn moods, Charles was the only one able to stir him out of it. When Charles left to go to Paris to prepare to enter the École Normale, Louis was devastated. He wrote to his friend: "The only pleasure left to me is to receive letters, those from you and those from my parents. Therefore, dear friend, write to me often."[4] Charles Chappuis remained a lifelong close friend to whom Louis often turned for advice and support in the most difficult times.

Louis studied hard at the school in Besançon, but his grades in history and geography were only mediocre, and in philosophy, Greek, Latin, and rhetoric they were just satisfactory. In all science courses, however, his grades were very good. Nevertheless, in August 1840 Louis received the degree of bachelor of letters. However, in order to qualify for the École Normale he would need a degree in science as well as in letters. Therefore he enrolled for a second year of study at the Besançon school.

To pay for his schooling, Louis tutored younger students in mathematics and physical science. In addition to three hundred francs per year, he received room and board. The three hundred francs was enough to pay for his tuition and for the firewood, the oil for lamps, and the candles he needed for his late-night studying. His parents sent preserved food to supplement his diet.

In those days of traveling mostly by carriage or on horseback, twenty-five miles was quite a long distance, so Louis went home for vacation only once or twice a year. Between visits he wrote letters to his family. Now that he had far surpassed his parents in education, he felt called upon to advise them about his sisters' education and to advise his sisters about their behavior. "Work hard, love one another," he told them. "These three things, Will, Work, Success, fill human existence. Will opens the door to success both brilliant and happy; Work passes these doors, and at the end of the journey Success comes to crown one's efforts."[5] Although his letters to them are filled with the preachy advice of a young man, they also show a tenderness and solicitude for his family. While he was still in school, Louis offered to take on additional tutoring duties to help send his sister Josephine to school, but his parents refused the offer.

Success Through Will and Work

During his second year at Besançon, Louis concentrated on science, which he enjoyed, and mathematics, which he hated. "Nothing dries up the heart so much as the study of mathematics,"[6] he wrote to his parents. Louis worked hard, but at the end of the year he failed to pass the examinations for the degree in science. To fail these tests was not unusual; more students who took them failed than passed. Many who failed dropped out of school. Louis, however, was determined to succeed. He signed up for another year at the school, worked harder, and passed the examinations. There was, however, one more hurdle to being admitted to the École Normale.

The École Normale accepted only the very best students in France, and every applicant was required to take grueling entrance exams that lasted for five days. Louis struggled through them and came out with a ranking of fifteen out of twenty-two students eligible for admission. Not satisfied with beginning as a low-ranking student, Louis decided to return to the preparatory school in Paris from which he had fled five years earlier. He was almost twenty years old now and had

As a young man, Pasteur was a very serious student who rarely indulged in the temptations of Parisian nightlife.

lived away from home for several years. This time he knew he would not succumb to homesickness.

The year in Paris proved to be a happy and profitable one. Louis was delighted to be reunited with his friend Charles Chappuis. They studied together and spent their leisure time exploring the city. Paris offered many temptations to young men, including wine, women, and bawdy stage shows. Louis reassured his parents that they were resisting the city's temptations. "When one wishes to keep straight, one can do so in this place as well as in any other; it is those who have no strength of will that succumb,"[7] he told them.

In order to pay part of his room and board, Louis again tutored younger students. In addition to the courses he was taking, he attended lectures at the prestigious Sorbonne University given by the well-known chemist Jean-Baptiste Dumas, who was also a senator and government minister. Dumas was a spellbinding lecturer who attracted as many as seven hundred students to each lecture, during which he expounded on the important work he had done in organic chemistry. Dumas inspired awe and devotion in young Louis.

The following summer, Louis took the École Normale entrance examinations again, and this time he scored so well he was ranked number four among those eligible for admission. Now he could enter the school with pride. Louis Pasteur moved into the dormitory of the École Normale in October 1843, eager to begin twelve-hour days of study, lectures, and laboratory work.

Chapter Two

THE ART OF CRYSTALLOGRAPHY

In October 1843, two months before Louis Pasteur's twenty-first birthday, he entered the École Normale eager to learn everything he could about chemistry and physics in order to become a first-rate teacher of these subjects. Pasteur quickly discovered that his greatest joy involved laboratory research aimed at answering questions that had puzzled scientists for hundreds of years. Of particular interest was the behavior of commonplace substances such as salt, sugar, and ice, all of which are made up of tiny structures called crystals.

The Excitement of Learning

Pasteur was in such a hurry to enter the École Normale that he arrived at the school days before the other students and slept in an empty dormitory. After classes began, he liked nothing more than spending his Sundays and holidays in the library or in the laboratory. He wrote home enthusiastically, praising his professors and describing the long hours he spent studying. His father was pleased that Louis found learning so exciting, but his intense concentration on his work disturbed the elder Pasteur. "You know how we worry about your health; you do work so immoderately," Jean-Joseph said. "Are you not injuring your eyesight by so much night work? Your ambition ought to be satisfied now you have reached your present position!"[8]

Jean-Joseph also wrote to Charles Chappuis (who was studying philosophy at the school), asking him to try to persuade Louis not to work so hard. The faithful Chappuis did his best. He waited patiently for his friend to finish an experiment and then dragged him out for long walks in the

Luxembourg Gardens. On these walks Chappuis talked about his professors and his classes in philosophy, while Pasteur shared his excitement about what he was learning and the experiments he was doing. Pasteur had a way of making his work sound interesting, and soon his philosopher friend was caught up in the world of crystals and their mysterious behavior when exposed to polarized light (light whose waves vibrate in only one plane). Chappuis believed his friend was a genius. "You will see what Pasteur will be,"[9] he often told others. Now, as he listened to Pasteur's ambitious dream of making discoveries that would startle the scientific world, Chappuis had complete faith that his friend would accomplish his goals.

Although he would have been happy to spend every day in the laboratory, Pasteur knew he had to concentrate on his coursework in order to pass the difficult final examinations that would earn him a teaching certificate. He did well: Out of a group of fourteen students, Pasteur was one of only four who passed the physics test. As soon as he was granted a teaching certificate, the Ministry of Education assigned him to teach physics at a secondary school in a small town. Pasteur, however, pleaded

A contemporary illustration shows Pasteur at work in his laboratory. Pasteur developed his lifelong love of laboratory experimentation while studying at the École Normale.

to be allowed to continue his research while he worked toward a doctoral degree at the École Normale. Antoine Balard, Pasteur's chemistry professor, took up his cause, declaring that it would be a shame to bury this promising young scientist in a tiny village. Balard bombarded the ministry officials with petitions until they yielded and agreed to allow Pasteur to remain at the school for another year of study while he also served as Balard's laboratory assistant.

The Balard Laboratory

Balard, who at the age of twenty-four had become famous for discovering bromine (the thirty-fifth element on the periodic table of elements), was an ideal mentor for Pasteur. In addition to being recognized as a brilliant chemist, Balard was known for his intensity and for his insistence on keeping the details of daily life as simple as possible in order to concentrate on his work. When he traveled, for example, his luggage consisted of a shirt and a pair of socks wrapped in newspaper and stuffed in his pocket. Balard had a bed set up in a corner of the laboratory, where he often spent his nights.

Balard believed that just as a worker should have a thorough understanding of his tools, a scientist should understand his lab equipment. Thus he encouraged his pupils to build for themselves as many of the instruments they needed as possible. He also encouraged them to do independent research. In this atmosphere Pasteur could satisfy his avid thirst to learn, to explore, and to discover.

Another fortunate circumstance for Pasteur was Auguste Laurent's arrival in Balard's laboratory. When Laurent, a well-respected scientist, asked Pasteur to collaborate with him on some experiments, Pasteur accepted with delight. He wrote to Chappuis, who was in Germany continuing his studies: "Even if the project should not produce any finding worth publishing, you can imagine that it would be very useful for me to do practical work for several months with such an experienced chemist. "However," he added, "during the summer I will try to do some other work by myself."[10]

There was plenty for Pasteur to do. To obtain his doctoral degree, he had to write two theses, or extended papers—one in chemistry and one in physics—and have them printed (a heavy expense). In his chemistry thesis titled "Researches into the Saturation Capacity of Arsenious Acid," Pasteur acknowledged the guidance he had received from Laurent and expressed his appreciation for "the kindly advice of a man so distinguished both by his talent and by his character."[11] In the physics thesis titled "Study of Phenomena Relative to the Rotatory Polarization of Liquids," Pasteur acknowledged the work that had been done by other scientists in the field and pointed out the importance of further studies in crystallography. Both theses he dedicated to his parents.

Pasteur received his doctor of science degree on August 28, 1847. Then he returned to Arbois to spend a few days with his family. Chappuis was urging him

In this laboratory at the École Normale, Pasteur conducted his earliest experiments in crystallography, the chemical science dealing with the structures of molecular crystals.

to come to Germany, tempting him by telling him he could study German from morning till night. Pasteur longed for just such an industrious holiday, since many important scientific papers were written in German and he would have liked to read the original texts rather than the translations. Nevertheless, he reluctantly told his friend that he could not afford the trip as the cost of having his theses printed had "ruined" him financially. Instead, Pasteur returned to Paris and Balard's lab-

oratory to continue the work he had begun in crystallography.

The First Scientific Triumph

Pasteur later explained some of the influences that had led to his interest in crystals:

> One day it happened that M. Laurent—studying if I mistake not, some tungstate of soda, perfectly crystallized—showed me through the

The Significance of Pasteur's First Discovery

In his biography Louis Pasteur, *distinguished French immunologist and physician Patrice Debré discusses the importance of Pasteur's first scientific discovery.*

In order to understand what makes Pasteur's discovery so important, one must of course go beyond the study of crystals and realize that Pasteur not only founded stereo-chemistry but also gave the initial impulse to developments that allowed biology to achieve greater advances in a few decades than had been made in several centuries.

In fact, Pasteur himself was one of the first to apply his discovery to physiology when he showed that the taste of food has to do with molecular asymmetry. While we are eating, molecules affect the nerve endings of the taste buds differently depending on whether they are right- or left-handed isomers. "When active dissymmetrical substances are involved in producing an impression on the nerves," he [Pasteur] wrote in this connection, "their effect is transferred by sweet taste in one case and almost no taste in the other."

Thanks to Pasteur, scientists thus began to see that in living beings molecules constitute the functional units of every organism. Forming the cells and the tissues, they mediate all biological events. To understand their organization opens the approach to their specific function. For the effect of every molecule depends on its connection to a receptor, as a key is connected to the lock it is designed to open. If one uses an inverse key, it will not work.

In discovering the principles of molecular asymmetry, Pasteur had done nothing less than to forge a key—and this key has unlocked the door to the whole of modern biology.

microscope, that this salt, apparently very pure, was evidently a mixture of three distinct kinds of crystals, easily recognizable with a little experience of crystalline forms. The lessons of our modest and excellent professor of mineralogy, M. Delafosse, had long since made me love crystallography. . . . I began to study carefully the formations of a very fine series of compounds, all very easily crystallized; tartaric acid and the tartrates. [12]

Pasteur focused on two kinds of crystals that formed in wine vats—tartaric acid and paratartaric, or racemic, acid. After it was purified, tartaric acid, a common by-product of wine making, was used in the dye industry, by pharmacists, and as an ingredient in baking powder. Racemic acid had the same chemical formula as tartaric but showed a striking difference in its optical activity. What this meant was that when a beam of light was passed through solutions of the two chemicals in a device called a polarimeter, the beam would bend in the tartaric acid solution but would not bend in the racemic acid solution. The famous German chemist Eilhardt Mitscherlich had reported to the French Academy of Sciences in Paris in 1844 that the crystalline forms of the two acids were identical. The puzzle Pasteur set out to solve was why—if the two acids had the same chemical formula and the same crystal structure—was tartaric acid optically active and racemic acid optically inactive?

Pasteur questioned Mitscherlich's conclusion. "To know how to wonder and to question is the first step of the mind toward discovery,"[13] he later recalled. To explore the problem, Pasteur set up a series of experiments. Working slowly and patiently, he spent long hours peering closely at the microscopic crystals of the two acids, making notes and drawings of what he was seeing.

Pasteur's experiments confirmed the work of other scientists that had shown that tartaric acid crystals were asymmetrical, with a tiny sloping facet in one corner, which explained why they were optically active. When he gazed closely at the crystals of racemic acid, however, he saw something other scientists had missed. Racemic acid crystals had the same slight asymmetry, but in some crystals the sloping facet was on the left side and in other crystals the facet was on the right side.

With his eyes glued to the microscope, Pasteur painstakingly separated the crystals into two piles—one containing the crystals with left-turning facets and the other the

An illustration shows Pasteur studying crystals in his laboratory. His crystallographic findings revealed how the shape of molecules influences their behavior.

crystals with right-turning facets. Then he dissolved each group in water and examined the solutions using the polarimeter. As he had expected, the solution of right-turning crystals turned polarized light to the right and the solution of left-turning crystals turned it to the left. When the solutions were mixed in equal amounts (as they were in racemic acid), the mixture was optically inactive; that is, it did not turn polarized light in either direction. Pasteur could not restrain his excitement at having solved the riddle. He rushed from the laboratory and grabbed the first person he met in the hall, an astonished physics assistant, and dragged him out into the Luxembourg Gardens to tell him about the great discovery he had made.

Recognition

Pasteur's work on racemic acid brought the twenty-five-year-old to the attention of the scientific world. Balard was extremely proud of his protégé and spread the news of his discovery. One of the most interested listeners was Jean-Baptiste Biot, a celebrated physicist who had discovered the optical activity of organic compounds and had invented the polarimeter. Like other good scientists, Biot had a "show me" attitude. He offered to attest to Pasteur's results if Pasteur would demonstrate his discovery under Biot's supervision. When Biot was satisfied that the results of the experiments were all that Pasteur had claimed, he said to him, "My dear boy, I have loved Science so much during my life, that this stirs my heart."[14]

As a result of this meeting, the seventy-four-year-old Biot became Pasteur's mentor and sponsor. Biot took every occasion to praise Pasteur publicly, recommended him for jobs, and introduced him to other eminent scientists. He also gave him fatherly advice against promoting his own work too enthusiastically. For example, when Pasteur proposed to write in an article that he would announce to the Academy of Sciences a finding "that deserves to command the highest degree of attention," Biot suggested he tone down his claim to read "which seems to me to be of considerable interest."[15] On another occasion, when Pasteur considered asking the academy or the president of France for funds he needed in order to travel to Saxony (Germany) to locate the rather scarce racemic acid for use in further experiments, Biot immediately offered to advance him the money, telling him it was not proper to bother the academy or the French president with such a request.

Pasteur would have liked nothing better than to spend every waking minute in the laboratory working with what he referred to as his "beautiful" crystals. However, in the year 1848 there were other important events that he could not ignore. His father's stories had long ago instilled in him a fierce patriotism. As a loyal Frenchman, therefore, he had to pay attention to political turmoil that threatened to turn his country upside down.

Beyond the Laboratory

The unrest that gripped the attention of Pasteur and much of France had been

Polarized Light

In addition to learning how to use the goniometer (an instrument that determines angles between crystal faces), Pasteur learned how to construct and use a polarimeter (a device used to quantify the rotation of light). Light waves normally travel in all directions from the source of the light. However, when light passes through a polarimeter, only certain rays—those parallel to each other and traveling in the same direction—can pass through. These parallel rays are called polarized light. By Pasteur's time, studies had already shown that some crystals bend polarized light as it passes through them. It was also known that some crystals (depending on their structure) bend light to the right and some bend light to the left.

building for some years. In 1830 French revolutionaries dissatisfied with the rule of King Charles X had placed Louis-Philippe on the throne. He was supposed to be the people's king, in sympathy with the middle classes; however, during Louis-Philippe's reign, harsh laws and indifference to the suffering of the people stirred unrest that resulted in another rebellion in 1848. Thousands of people roamed the streets of Paris. Reports of killings and arrests alarmed Pasteur's family, who feared for his safety. Pasteur himself, however, was reveling in the excitement. He sided with the rebels and gave all of his savings to the cause. He also joined the National Guard. "If it became necessary, I would fight with the greatest courage for the sacred cause of the Republic,"[16] he wrote to his family.

As concerned as Pasteur was over the political situation, an even greater worry was the news that he received in May that his mother was very ill. He rushed to Arbois, but arrived too late. Jeanne Pasteur had died of a massive stroke. For weeks Pasteur was unable to work as he tried to comfort his stricken family, all the while brooding over whether worry about his safety might have caused his mother's illness. Eventually he did return to the laboratory, finding release from his troubles by intensely concentrating on his research.

Pasteur had little time to devote to that research, however. Although Paris was in chaos, the Ministry of Education was still overseeing the nation's schools, and it now informed Pasteur that it was time for him to assume his teaching duties. He was assigned to teach physics in the city of Dijon, in east-central France. Though Pasteur liked teaching he hated the long hours he had to spend preparing lessons and grading the papers of sometimes as many as eighty students in a class.

The Laboratories of Paris

The laboratories in which Pasteur worked in the early days of his career were nothing like what comes to mind when we think of a laboratory today. There were no tiled floors, overhead lights, gleaming counters and sinks, temperature controls, or rows of up-to-date equipment. Even the greatest French scientists worked in cramped, often dimly lit, stuffy, smelly, unhealthy spaces. Sometimes the so-called laboratory was in a cellar or an attic or a corner of a lumber room. Often the state made no provision at all for doing laboratory work. Even a famous scientist such as J.B. Dumas had to make his own arrangements. Rather than work in the dismal room reserved for him at the Sorbonne, he converted space in his own house into a laboratory. Few scientists, and certainly no poor student like Pasteur, had the private means to establish a suitable working place in which to do experiments. It is all the more astonishing then that Pasteur accomplished all that he did under the conditions in which he worked.

The laboratories in which Pasteur worked were dimly lit, poorly ventilated, and supplied with primitive equipment.

After two months performing this disagreeable work he was happy to receive news that he had been appointed to a higher position as a professor of chemistry at the University of Strasbourg.

Meanwhile, the revolt that had begun in February was coming to an end. In December the French people elected Louis-Napoleon (nephew of Emperor Napoleon Bonaparte) president. Louis-Napoleon's interest in industry and science would be of benefit to Pasteur in his future work. Pasteur was about to begin an exciting new phase of his career. Even more important to his future, he was about to meet the woman who would become his wife.

Chapter Three

The World of the "Infinitely Small"

Pasteur's first important discovery made possible a better understanding of the structure of crystals, and he believed that in time further research into crystallography would reveal hidden truths about the nature of all living things. For the rest of his life Pasteur continued to talk about the possibilities of important revelations through further experiments with crystals, but events directed his attention elsewhere. The shift of his research interests from crystallography to fermentation led to discoveries about microorganisms that would prove to be of major importance.

The Perfect Wife

In January 1849 Pasteur took up his duties as acting professor of chemistry at the University of Strasbourg and began one of the happiest periods of his life. Before the move, Pasteur had written to his father that, since he had no plans to marry, he might ask one of his sisters to come live with him and keep house for him. Very soon, however, his plans changed dramatically.

Soon after his arrival in Strasbourg, Pasteur was invited to a reception at the home of Charles Laurent, the head of the university. At this gathering he met Marie, Laurent's twenty-two-year-old daughter. Apparently Pasteur decided almost immediately that Marie would be the ideal wife for him. Although they could hardly have met more than a few times in formal gatherings, less than a month after his arrival in Strasbourg, Pasteur wrote to Charles Laurent, asking permission to marry his daughter. With typical directness, Pasteur set about achieving his goal of marrying Marie.

In his businesslike letter of February 10 to Marie's father, Pasteur included details that he explained "may have some weight in determining your acceptance or refusal." He described his family background, including his father's tanning business in Arbois, adding, "I do not value what we possess at more than fifty thousand francs, and I have long ago decided to hand over my share to my sisters. I have therefore absolutely no fortune. My only means are good health, some courage, and my position in the University." Pasteur also mentioned his degrees, his ambition to be elected a member of the Academy of Sciences, his love of science, and his desire to be able to devote himself "entirely to chemical research" in the future. He told Laurent that his father would come to Strasbourg to make the proposal of marriage, and added a postscript: "I was twenty-six on December 27."[17]

Pasteur also wrote to Marie's mother, humbly telling her: "There is nothing in me to attract a young girl's fancy. But my recollections tell me that those who have known me very well have loved me very much." To Marie he wrote, "All that I beg of you, Mademoiselle, is that you will not judge me too hastily, and therefore misjudge me. Time will show you that below my cold, shy and unpleasing exterior, there is a heart full of affection for you."[18]

At the University of Strasbourg, Pasteur worked as a professor of chemistry and directed the activities of a busy laboratory like this one.

Apparently Pasteur's exterior was not too unpleasing to Marie, for she married her impetuous suitor on May 29, 1849. It was soon apparent that Pasteur could not have made a better choice. From the beginning of their marriage Marie accepted that Pasteur's work in the laboratory came before everything else. She not only took care of all the domestic problems and protected him from unwanted interruptions, but also served as his secretary and collaborator. Her interest in his work was genuine; in the evenings when he dictated to her, she asked him to explain exactly why he was doing certain experiments and what he hoped to learn from them.

Marie also learned not to make any plans herself. When a grand parade took place in Strasbourg to honor a visit by Louis-Napoleon, Pasteur promised his wife that he would go with her to see it. Even when he broke that promise so that he could finish an experiment, Marie was understanding. The only times she scolded him were when she felt his long hours in the laboratory were endangering his health. She regarded her hardworking husband with a mixture of common sense and wry humor. In a letter to her father-in-law, she said, "Louis . . . always worries a little too much about his experiments. You know that those he is planning for this year are supposed to give us, if they are successful, a Newton or a Galileo."[19]

During the Pasteurs' five years in Strasbourg, three of their children were born: Jeanne in 1850, Jean-Baptiste in 1851, and Cecile in 1853. Pasteur was a good and loving father, although often an absent one, for he put in long hours preparing lectures and continuing his exploration of crystal formulations in the laboratory.

The Strasbourg Years

Despite the heavy demands of his teaching duties, Pasteur managed to greatly expand his work on optical activity and crystalline asymmetry while he was in Strasbourg. In 1851 he wrote to his friend Chappuis that he felt he was on the verge of uncovering mysteries. He also complained that the nights were too long as the necessity of sleep kept him away from the laboratory.

When his supply of racemic acid, which he needed to carry out his experiments, ran low, Pasteur undertook a strenuous trip to Germany and Austria to try to discover a source for it. What he discovered was that some unrefined tartar, wherever it is found, contains racemic acid. The refining process destroys it. Therefore, he concluded, the reason the French preparations of tartaric acid contained no racemic acid was due to the manufacturing processes in France.

Back in Strasbourg, Pasteur conducted a series of experiments until he finally discovered how to produce racemic acid from tartaric acid by a process using heat and additional chemicals. In other words, he had found a way to synthesize racemic acid—something other scientists had been trying to do for many years. Thrilled by this discovery, Pasteur telegraphed a succinct message to Biot: "Transforming tar-

The Perfect Helpmate

Marie Laurent was a graceful, blue-eyed young woman of twenty-two at the time of her marriage to Louis Pasteur. She had a sweet voice and liked to sing as she went about her work. Her happy nature, sense of humor, and keen mind proved to be great assets to her serious husband. In Louis Pasteur: Free Lance of Science, *René Dubos quotes Pasteur's associate of twenty years, Émile Roux, who described the Pasteurs' relationship.*

From the first days of their common life, Madame Pasteur understood what kind of man she had married; she did everything to protect him from the difficulties of life, taking onto herself the worries of the home that he might retain the full freedom of his mind for his investigations. Madame Pasteur loved her husband to the extent of understanding his studies. During the evenings, she wrote under his dictation, calling for explanations, for she took a genuine interest in crystalline structure or attenuated viruses. She had become aware that ideas become the clearer for being explained to others, and that nothing is more conducive to devising new experiments than describing the ones which have just been completed. Madame Pasteur was more than an incomparable companion for her husband, she was his best collaborator.

taric acid into racemic acid. Please inform Dumas . . . Pasteur."[20]

The Society of Pharmacy of Paris was delighted with this breakthrough and awarded Pasteur a fifteen-hundred-franc prize. With Marie's consent he used half of the prize money to purchase laboratory equipment that the university did not supply. Thanks to the efforts of highly influential friends like Biot, Dumas, and Balard, Pasteur received another prestigious honor in 1853, when he was named Chevalier de la Legion d'Honneur. Now both father and son could wear the red ribbon of the Legion of Honor on their lapels.

A New Line of Research

A third honor awarded to Pasteur marked another turning point in his life. The Faculty of Sciences at the newly created university at Lille, the fifth largest city in France, was in need of a dean. Located in the heart of a booming industrial region with a number of factories and distilleries, the school was intended to turn out graduates who could apply their knowledge of scientific principles as factory managers and industrial chemists. The Ministry of Education chose as dean Louis Pasteur, whose publications on crystallography had been so impressive. The fact that Pasteur had come up with

As a professor, Pasteur devoted as much attention to preparing his lectures as he did to carrying out his experiments.

a practical result in synthesizing racemic acid proved he could apply scientific theories to achieve practical results. The fact that he believed in having his students do a lot of laboratory work was also a factor in the ministry's decision.

For Pasteur the appointment as professor of chemistry and dean of the Faculty of Sciences in December 1854 meant a promotion and an increase in salary. It also meant a change in his working goals. From that point forward he was no longer dedicated just to pure science and the pursuit of theoretical objectives; in Lille he experienced the excitement of using his genius to solve practical problems for industry. He warned his faculty and students, however, against thinking that pure and applied science were two different things. There was only science, he told them, and the application of science.

Pasteur was an enthusiastic teacher who had the ability to instill in others his fascination with science. Soon after his arrival in Lille he spoke to a group of manufacturers and parents of students asking, "Where will you find a young man whose curiosity and interest will not immediately be awakened when you put into his hands a potato, when with that potato he produces sugar, with that sugar, alcohol, with that alcohol ether and vinegar?"[21] In his inaugural address at the university he repeated his favorite formula for success: "In the fields of observation, chance only favors the mind which is prepared."[22] Pasteur not

Microbes

A microbe, or microorganism, is a living being that is so small it can be seen only through a microscope. Most microbes consist of only one cell and are less than one-tenth of a millimeter long.

Yeasts are microbes that, like mushrooms, belong to the group of plants called fungi. They may multiply in two ways. Some yeasts form new plants by forming buds, which break off from the parent plant to form independent cells. Other yeasts increase by fission, a process in which they simply divide in two. Much of Pasteur's work was with yeasts used in the production of alcohol, beer, and wine.

Bacteria are any of a large group of microorganisms. They can live almost anywhere and multiply rapidly under favorable conditions. Bacteria may be harmful, causing diseases and spoilage of foods, or they may be useful, like those that live in our bodies and aid in the digestion of food. A germ, in popular use, is a microbe that causes harm. Therefore, some bacteria are called germs.

only prepared his students through lectures and experiments but also took them on tours of factories in neighboring towns and as far away as Belgium for firsthand observations of manufacturing processes.

Fermentation and the Life Force

It was Pasteur's own well-prepared mind and his previous work with crystals that enabled him to tackle and solve problems that threatened to destroy some of the most important industries in France. The fermentation of beet sugar for the production of pure alcohol was one of the most important businesses in the region around Lille. In the summer of 1856, M. Bigo, the father of one of Pasteur's students and the owner of a factory, asked Pasteur if he could help

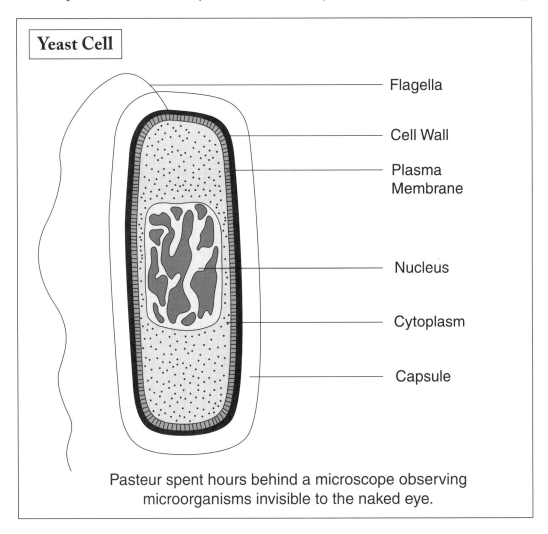

Yeast Cell

Flagella

Cell Wall

Plasma Membrane

Nucleus

Cytoplasm

Capsule

Pasteur spent hours behind a microscope observing microorganisms invisible to the naked eye.

him solve a serious difficulty he was having in manufacturing alcohol by fermenting beet-root juice. Often, Bigo told Pasteur, his fermentations turned sour; that is, they yielded lactic acid instead of alcohol. And he said the same problem was plaguing other distillers. Pasteur was intrigued by the mystery, and he undertook the challenge of solving it with all of his insatiable curiosity and indefatigable energy. Marie Pasteur wrote to her father-in-law, "Louis . . . is now up to his neck in beet juice. He spends all his days in the distillery. He has probably told you that he teaches only one lecture a week; this leaves him much free time which, I assure you, he uses and abuses."[23]

Pasteur knew there were two theories about the cause of fermentation and decay in organic material, one that was chemical and one biological. Many eminent scientists believed both these processes (fermentation and decay) resulted purely from a chemical reaction; a handful of other scientists, however, held that there was a biological cause. They believed that fermentation was caused by microorganisms, or minute plants or animals that are invisible to the naked eye. Pasteur, too, believed in this theory and set out to prove it.

As Marie had told Jean-Joseph, Pasteur was indeed spending much of his time at distilleries. He even created a small laboratory in the cellar of M. Bigo's factory where he could study samples taken from the fermenting vats at different stages. He set up his simple student's microscope

and his flasks and other equipment necessary for carrying out experiments.

Pasteur was remarkably patient when it came to performing endless experiments until he was satisfied with his results. He was willing to try as many different approaches as it took to find the one that worked. During countless hours of analyzing, cultivating, incubating, and examining samples taken from the good and bad vats in the distilleries, there were many times of disappointment when he wrote in his notebook, "mistake . . . all wrong . . . no."[24]

Solving the Mystery

Finally, Pasteur found clues that helped him solve the mystery of why some fermenting juices spoiled while others did not. On the slides where he had dropped liquid from the vats that were producing good alcohol, there were tiny globules of yeast with buds sprouting from their sides. These tiny plants were obviously alive and well. In the samples from the spoiled vats, however, where there was lactic acid instead of alcohol, he found specks that turned out to be tangles of tiny rods that appeared to be in constant vibration. Pasteur had a theory that the juice in the vats spoiled because the rod-shaped objects were alive and overran the yeast cells and kept them from making alcohol. He set out to prove this theory.

To really study the little rods, Pasteur had to find a way of growing them in a clear liquid. He concocted different kinds of liquids that he hoped the rods might

Fermentation

Fermentation is a natural process, and there is no record of when humans first observed it and began to make use of it. In ancient times they learned to make wine from grapes, vinegar from wine or hard cider, bread from starchy paste, and cheese from milk. They also took advantage of the fact that fodder stored in silos fermented into silage, a juicy food for their livestock. In addition to cheeses, people enjoyed fermented foods such as sauerkraut, buttermilk, and dill pickles. Most people accepted the changes that created these blessings without questioning their cause. Some philosophers and scientists, however, wondered why grape juice bubbled in vintners' vats, why wine sometimes turned into vinegar, and why adding yeast to flour paste caused it to rise.

By the nineteenth century enough studies had been done to show that there were different kinds of fermentation. Decay or putrefaction, characterized by the fetid odor of rotten eggs or meat and other decomposing organic matter, was included in the definition of fermentation. Among the types of fermentation that Pasteur studied were alcoholic, resulting in wine and beer; acetic, resulting in vinegar; lactic, resulting in soured milk; and butyric, resulting in the rancid taste of spoiled butter.

After his preliminary work on fermentation, Pasteur would continue to study the process for twenty years, expanding on his early generalizations but always defending his doctrine that fermentation is caused by the vital processes of living organisms.

find nourishing and grow in, but nothing seemed to work. After many failures, Pasteur tried a broth made from boiled and strained dried yeast with a little sugar and carbonate of chalk (which kept the solution from being too acidic). Carefully lifting a speck with a fine needle, he placed it in a bottle of the yeast broth and put the bottle in an incubating oven.

In between teaching classes, conducting laboratory demonstrations, and eating and sleeping (at Marie's insistence), Pasteur hurried back to examine the bottle. For two days nothing happened. He began to think this was another failure. Then one evening as he held the bottle up to the dim light in the laboratory and squinted at it, he saw bubbles rising from a spiral of gray cloud that had formed in the bottle. Quickly he took a drop from the bottle and peered at it through his microscope. It was teeming with the tiny vibrating rods. He knew now that the rods were living organisms and that they could reproduce themselves. To confirm his findings, he repeated the same experiment over and over. After it had worked time after time and he had produced billions of rods, Pasteur was ready to tell the world what he had discovered about the "infinitely small" creatures that could do a huge amount of harm. He was confident that they were the villains that destroyed yeast and produced lactic acid.

Continuing the Search

Although Pasteur often referred to himself as being shy and modest, he was actually an excellent public relations person whenever he felt he had something important to make known. Now, he told his classes and his colleagues about his discovery; wrote letters to his faithful mentors, Dumas and Biot; dictated scientific papers to Marie for publication; and made presentations before learned scientific societies.

Pasteur was well aware that there was still much to learn about the complicated

A scientist examines bacteria specimens. Pasteur worked hard to isolate the bacteria that spoils alcohol.

process of fermentation and about the different kinds of fermentation and putrefaction. He had discovered the reason for bad fermentations in the beet-root vats, but he could not yet tell the distillers how to avoid the spoilage other than to examine the liquid under the microscope as he had done and then to throw out any found to contain the deadly rods.

After this first research on microbes, which brought him acclaim from the scientific community, Pasteur could have stopped. It was not his way, however, to let a problem go until he had used every means he could think of to solve it. He wanted to do more than just explain the cause of the spoilage that occurred during fermentations. He wanted to find a way to prevent it from happening.

Chapter Four

NOT A MINUTE TO SPARE

P asteur's ideas regarding the causes of fermentation and its failure quickly gained acceptance, bringing him much acclaim. Pasteur, however, saw that the practical application of his theory would be in preventing that failure. In pursuing that goal, Pasteur changed the lives of countless people.

Return to Paris

Although the years Pasteur spent in Strasbourg and Lille were happy and rewarding, Paris was *the* great scientific center, so when an opportunity to return to that city presented itself, he took it. On October 22, 1857, at the age of thirty-four, Pasteur was appointed administrator and director of scientific studies at the École Normale Supérieure. Although he preferred to spend his time in the laboratory, Pasteur conscientiously carried out his administrative

duties. He was involved not only with finances and curriculum but with almost every aspect of student life, including overseeing the food service, sanitary facilities, and the condition of buildings. He also had to deal with the school's relationship with parents and with the discipline of the students.

As the director of scientific studies, Pasteur made lasting improvements in the system at his alma mater. He shifted the emphasis from training teachers to training researchers. He encouraged the students and graduates of the school to write scientific papers and founded and edited a journal to publish those papers. He also recruited several of the brightest students to help carry on his research, and provided to students who had obtained their degrees opportunities for temporary employment at the school.

Pasteur's means of relaxing from his lecturing and administrative duties was to do research. Since his laboratory was adjacent to his living quarters, it was easy for him to spend his spare time carrying out experiments. In the evenings Marie copied letters and reports and manuscripts for him. The Pasteurs rarely attended social events, and their vacations were simply a few days spent at the seashore.

In 1857 Pasteur was appointed administrator and director of sciences at the École Normale Supérieure, his alma mater.

Family Life

The birth of another daughter, Marie-Louise, in 1858 was a happy event for the Pasteurs, but it was soon followed by a series of family tragedies. In August 1859 while Marie was on a visit to Arbois with the children, their oldest daughter, Jeanne, was stricken with typhoid fever. The best physicians available were consulted, and Marie sent word to Pasteur that the child was improving. But Jeanne suddenly suffered a relapse and died on September 10, before Pasteur could reach Arbois.

After the funeral, Pasteur returned to Paris alone. For some time he was so filled with grief he could hardly speak. His only solace was in his work and in his love for his family. While Marie was still in Arbois, he wrote to her:

> Yes, when you come back, I wish that between us, with us, there will be nothing but our love, our children, their upbringing, their future, along with my dreams of science. For you, for them, life will be made beautiful by my work, by the success of new discoveries, and by generous feelings. [25]

The birth of the Pasteurs' fifth child, Camille, in 1863 brought new joy to the parents, but it was short lived. The baby developed a liver tumor and survived for only two years. Camille's body was taken to Arbois, where she was buried beside her sister.

That same year, 1865, Pasteur's father also died. After the funeral in Arbois,

Working at the École

When Pasteur began teaching at the École Normale Supérieure in Paris in 1857, there were no laboratories for professors, so he used his ingenuity to create one out of two tiny attic rooms at the school. Even though he was unable to stand up straight in the cramped space, Pasteur was determined to continue his experiments on fermentation. A year later he obtained permission to set up a laboratory in a small detached building near the school gates. It was better than the attic space—but not by much. The incubating oven was in a cubbyhole under the stairs, so the dignified scientist had to crawl on his hands and knees to get to it. He was not given a budget for equipment, and he had to ask for money every year or find a way to skim it from the general budget.

Pasteur sat in an empty room above the tannery and wrote a long letter to Marie. In it he recalled his father's loving care, his guidance, and the example he had set for hard work and family loyalty. "My dear father," he wrote, "how thankful I am that I could give him some satisfaction!"[26]

The following year the Pasteurs suffered yet another tragedy when their daughter Cecile was stricken with typhoid fever. Again, just when it was thought she was recovering, she suffered a relapse and died. Pasteur again arrived too late to see his daughter before she died. Stunned by this series of family tragedies, he fell into a brief period of despair. He was afraid that all of their children would die before they grew up, and he expressed the wish that he too could die. This depression, however, did not last long. As always, Marie's courage helped him bear his grief, and as always his work, with its possibilities of new discoveries, spurred him on.

The Great Debate

The series of deaths in his family and the death of his beloved mentor Biot, which had occurred in 1862, made Pasteur more aware of his own mortality. He complained that twenty-four-hour days were not long enough, saying, "The life of a scientist is so short! So numerous are the mysteries of nature, especially of living nature!"[27] He declared that between his administrative duties, his teaching, and his research he had not a minute to spare. Although this statement would seem to have been true, Pasteur nevertheless found time to enter into one of the hottest controversies of the day.

The battle Pasteur chose to enter involved the controversy over the theory of spontaneous generation. This theory, which held that living things could spring from nothing, had been around for a long time when Pasteur decided to tackle it. Several of his scientist friends, including Dumas, discouraged him from entering the battlefield, believing he would be wasting his time since, over the years, many scientists had tried and failed to prove or disprove the idea. Pasteur did not agree. In 1860 the Academy of Sciences had offered a cash prize to any scientist who succeeded in meeting the challenge "to attempt, by carefully conducted experiments, to throw new light on the question of the so-called spontaneous generation."[28] Louis Pasteur accepted that challenge.

Pasteur did not actually set out to disprove the existence of spontaneous generation. Indeed, from the beginning he acknowledged that somewhere in the universe life might be creating itself. Instead, he sought simply to debunk the claims of those who said they had brought about conditions under which spontaneous generation occurred. Still, he knew that if he were successful, the social and scientific implications of his feat would be tremendously important.

For Pasteur, his interest was the natural outgrowth of his work on fermentation. He explained,

Among the questions raised by my research on the ferments in the narrow sense, none are more worthy of attention than those relating to the origin of the ferments. Where do they come from, these mysterious agents, so feeble in appearance yet so powerful in reality, which, with minimal weight and insignificant external chemical characteristics, possess exceptional energy? This is the problem that has led me to study the so-called spontaneous generations.[29]

The Swan-Necked Flasks

The scientist whose work Pasteur singled out to oppose most rigorously was Felix-Archimede Pouchet, a respected naturalist. Pouchet had published a book in 1859 in which he espoused acceptance of the theory of spontaneous generation. The correspondence between Pasteur and Pouchet began politely and privately but became more heated as the debate continued and each man made his conclusions public. At first, Pasteur apologized for telling Pouchet what he thought on "so delicate a subject," which he said he had not yet studied thoroughly. He then advised Pouchet that if he would repeat his experiments with proper precautions he would find that "in your recent experiments you have unwittingly introduced [contaminated] common air, so that the conclusions to which you have come are not founded on facts of irreproachable exactitude."[30] In other words, Pasteur was finding fault with Pouchet's experimental methods.

Pouchet and his supporters replied to Pasteur's claim of the existence of germs in the air by saying that, if this were true, the air would be so heavily laden with living microorganisms that it would be dark and as dense as iron. To answer this ridiculous objection and prove that microbes are to be found in dust, Pasteur constructed an experiment that involved sterilizing a liquid broth and keeping it sterile until he was ready to expose it to air. Pasteur and his assistants prepared a large number of swan-neck flasks, glass containers with long necks that were curved in an S shape, for a dramatic demonstration. Sugared yeast-water was sterilized by boiling it in the flasks, which were then sealed by melting the glass at the tip of the neck. By doing this, Pasteur could assure himself that the growth medium inside would not be in contact with air until he was ready.

Then Pasteur and his helpers left the laboratory and became explorers in search of dust particles. In various places they took samples by carefully snapping the end of the necks of the flasks, allowing air to rush in and then resealing and incubating them. The results of these experiments proved that the air in the various environments varied greatly in its purity. In the still air captured in an unused cellar, there was almost no dust and almost no microbes; nine out of the ten bottles were clear. In the samples of air taken in a Paris courtyard, on the other hand, all of the bottles soon swarmed with microscopic living creatures.

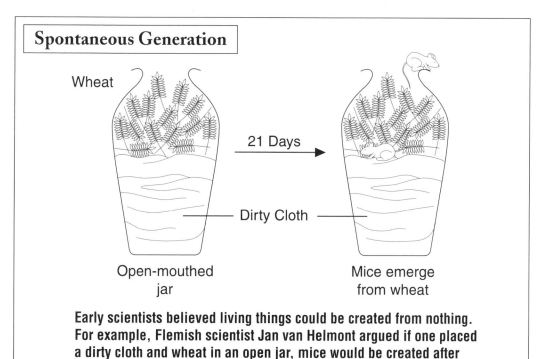

Spontaneous Generation

Wheat

21 Days

Dirty Cloth

Open-mouthed jar

Mice emerge from wheat

Early scientists believed living things could be created from nothing. For example, Flemish scientist Jan van Helmont argued if one placed a dirty cloth and wheat in an open jar, mice would be created after twenty-one days. However, van Helmont did not consider the fact that the mice had wandered into the jar for an easy meal.

Farther afield, Pasteur tested the air in his hometown of Arbois. It was cleaner than Paris air. He tested the air in the foothills of the Alps, and eight of twenty flasks showed contamination. Finally, he climbed a mountain in the Alps with twenty flasks strapped to the back of a mule. Only one of the flasks that he opened in the cold, clear air and then resealed later showed the presence of microbes.

Although a few proponents of the theory of spontaneous generation still refused to let go of their beliefs, Pasteur was satisfied that he had proven that it takes life (in this case microorganisms) to create life. On the evening of April 7, 1864, in the large auditorium of the Sorbonne, he gave a public lecture in which he reported his findings. In the packed audience were famous literary figures and socialites as well as scientists, professors, and students. Word had gone out that this would be a dramatic presentation during which important truths would be revealed, and the audience was not disappointed. Pasteur outlined the history of the controversy over spontaneous generation. He explained his experiments and showed his audience the swan-neck flasks he had used. He ended by showing them a flask in which the con-

Spontaneous Generation

The idea that living things can spring into being from nonliving substances began as a myth to explain certain mysteries. Ancient civilizations believed that bees arose without parents from the entrails of dead bulls and that eels arose without parents from the mud of rivers. As late as the sixteenth century, a famous physiologist announced that he could create mice by placing a few grains of wheat or a piece of cheese in a cloth. In a few days the mice would appear, he declared, and furthermore, they would be fully grown.

By Pasteur's time, scientists no longer believed in the spontaneous generation of mice or eels. Many, however, still believed that small creatures could simply spring into being. Although experiments had shown that if flies were kept away from meat, no maggots would appear (since no larva-producing eggs would have been laid), there were still many skeptics. Particularly hard to overcome was the idea that invisible microorganisms sprang into being spontaneously. Pasteur was one of those who believed that microbes bred microbes. In his painstaking way, through trial and error, he set out to disprove the theory of spontaneous generation.

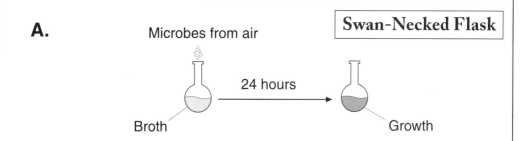

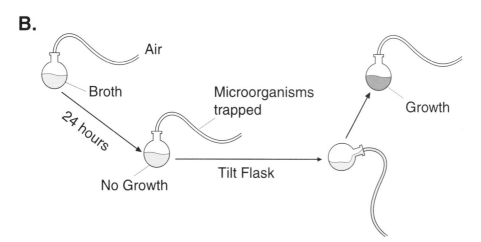

Experiment A shows that when broth is exposed to air, microbes will grow in the broth.

In B, Pasteur demonstrated that swan-necked flasks would trap the microbes, preventing the broth from being contaminated. When the flask was tilted, putting the broth in contact with the microorganisms in the neck, growth occurred.

tents were still sterile after many years, telling them:

I could point to that liquid and say to you, I have taken my drop of water from the immensity of creation, and I have taken it full of the elements appropriated to the development of inferior beings. And I wait, I watch, I question it!—begging it to recommence for me the beautiful spectacle of the first creation. But it is dumb, dumb since these experiments were begun several years ago; it is dumb because I have kept it from the only thing man does not know how to produce: from the germs which float in the air, from Life, for Life is a germ and a germ is Life. Never will the doctrine of spontaneous generation recover from the mortal blow of this simple experiment. [31]

Through the wide publicity given this and other public lectures and the attention given by the news media to various articles by Pasteur in scientific journals, his name was becoming well known to the general public—as well as to the ruling powers of France.

Pasteurization

It was not long before Pasteur had an opportunity to apply what he had learned from his experiments. The wine trade, so important to the French economy, was in deep trouble in the early 1860s. English merchants, who imported large quantities of French wine, were canceling orders, complaining that the wine they were buying was

Pasteur's method of treating food with heat to kill undesirable microorganisms helps to preserve milk, cheese, wine, and other foods that easily spoil.

Pasteur and Napoleon III

Pasteur relished recognition by prominent people. Napoleon III (a nephew of Napoleon Bonaparte) was the last member of the Bonaparte family to rule France. He and his wife, Empress Eugenie, sometimes invited outstanding scientists, as well as writers and painters, to spend time at their royal residences. In the autumn of 1865 Pasteur was asked to spend a week at the grand royal chateau at Compiègne. He was very pleased and flattered by the attention he received from the royal couple.

Pasteur wrote to Marie, describing in detail the decor of the rooms, the appearance of the beautiful empress, and the dinner menus. He was delighted, he told his wife, to find that Eugenie knew about his work, and he described a lively conversation in which they discussed microbes, cholera, and the diseases of French wine. Complying with a request from the emperor, Pasteur set up his microscope and showed members of the court the wicked microbes that were causing the problems for the wine makers.

In *Louis Pasteur*, Patrice Debré quotes Pasteur's advice to his son Jean-Baptiste following the visit: "The honor of spending a week in the Emperor's company which I have just received will make you understand the rewards of hard work and good conduct. You should therefore also work hard, so that one day, God willing, you may have the same satisfaction."

often sour or bitter and sometimes looked oily. And at home, most French householders, who would not think of having a meal without wine, frequently expressed disappointment in its quality. General Ildephonse Fave, aide-de-camp to the emperor, Napoleon III (also known as Louis-Napoleon), suggested that Pasteur be commissioned to study the wine problem, and the emperor, who was eager to help the wine industry, agreed.

Flattered by the imperial request, Pasteur quickly set to work. His hometown of Arbois was famous for its wines, and it was there that he set up a makeshift laboratory to examine the good and bad wines that his old childhood friends brought to him. He also inspected the fermentation practices in other wine-producing locales and listened to the winemakers who described the so-called alterations in their wines. He concluded that although many variables, such as how the wine was handled and stored, could affect a wine's taste, most of the problems could be traced to harmful microorganisms. To rid the wines of these unwanted microorganisms, Pasteur began treating wine with heat. He found that when the finished wines were heated for an hour to

55 degrees centigrade (131 degrees Fahrenheit), the harmful microorganisms were significantly reduced in number. Wine treated in this way could be stored indefinitely, and the taste was not affected.

This process of partial sterilization, which became known as pasteurization, was soon used not just for wine but for a wide range of drinks and foods. In addition to wine, vinegar, and beer, it was used to treat milk and cheese and other foods that had long been vulnerable to spoiling. Thanks to Pasteur's insight, industries quickly adopted this method of preserving their products, and people around the world benefited by having safer foods and drinks. The term *pasteurization* became a household word, and Louis Pasteur was honored as a benefactor of humankind.

Chapter Five

Saving the Silk Industry

As Pasteur's reputation grew, so did demands on his time. Many organizations wanted to honor him; various groups wanted him to give lectures; editors wanted him to write articles. With his incredible energy, Pasteur was able to fulfill many of these demands and still focus on solving scientific problems that concerned him deeply. Despite family tragedies and his own health problems, he labored tirelessly to apply what he had learned to the benefit of France.

A Decent Laboratory

In 1867 Pasteur received a great honor when the position formerly held by his old friend and mentor Antoine Balard, professor of chemistry at the Sorbonne, was offered to him. Pasteur eagerly accepted; he requested, however, that the Ministry of Education also construct a new, well-equipped laboratory at the École Normale where he could continue his research. In his request he appealed to the patriotism of his fellow countrymen, stressing "the importance of carrying out studies of immense practical importance, particularly on infectious diseases," and pointing out "the necessity of maintaining the scientific superiority of France against the efforts of rival nations."[32]

Emperor Louis-Napoleon supported Pasteur's request, and construction of the new, large laboratory began in August 1868. In accordance with Pasteur's wishes, it was to be connected with the Pasteurs' private living quarters. When he was urged to take time off from work for pleasure, Pasteur always said that his work *was* his pleasure, and he liked to live as close to his work as possible.

In 1867 Pasteur accepted the chemistry professorship at the Sorbonne on the condition that the French government provide him with a state-of-the-art laboratory at the École Normale.

Beginning Silkworm Research

Meanwhile, Pasteur had received a new challenge. Southern France had long been home to a thriving silk production industry. However, something was killing the tiny caterpillars that produced the fibers from which silk was spun. Pasteur was intrigued when, in 1865, his mentor and longtime friend Jean-Baptiste Dumas (now a senator) asked him to investigate the epidemic. Yet Pasteur saw one basic impediment. He replied, "Consider, I pray you, that I have never even touched a silkworm."[33] Dumas persisted, however, pleading that Pasteur would be performing a great service to his country. Unable to resist this appeal from his mentor, Pasteur agreed to accept the challenge. A month later, he had touched a great many silkworms and had embarked on a lengthy project.

Accompanied by four students, Pasteur traveled to Dumas's hometown of Alais (spelled Ales today) near the Mediterranean Sea. The silk industry had been established in this region in the Middle Ages when silkworms and the mulberry trees on which they fed were brought there from China. The worms thrived and by the mid-1800s France was producing a tenth of the world's silk. In the Alais region the silk industry was a major economic force. It was not just confined to large manufacturers. Many individuals were deeply involved in the cultivation of mulberry trees, and there were numerous small, family-owned silkworm nurseries where the men harvested the mulberry leaves and the women and children watched over the worms. The people called the disease that was killing the silkworms *pebrine*, a local word for pepper, because the sick worms were covered with black spots.

By reading, listening, and observing, Pasteur soon knew a great deal about the life cycle of the silkworm. He learned that the so-called silkworm was actually the caterpillar, or larva, of a white moth with black-lined wings. He also found that whereas wild silk moths laid their seed-like eggs in mulberry trees and the worms were left to take care of themselves, the

Pasteur as Disciplinarian

Although Pasteur was a successful administrator, he was not as successful in handling matters of student discipline. At the École Normale he especially locked horns with the students in the humanities, who, perhaps, did not have the great respect for his genius that those enrolled in the sciences did. Pasteur would not tolerate insubordination, and he expelled students who left the school grounds without permission or were caught smoking. Like his father, Pasteur could be rigid and authoritarian when he believed he was morally right.

In 1867 an outright rebellion occurred at the school when a Paris newspaper published a letter by a student supporting a liberal senator. The student letter-writer was suspended, since school regulations forbade any political activity. When Pasteur demanded to know the names of the two students who had taken the letter to the newspaper, the students walked out en masse and protested by marching through the streets. The school was forced to close, and when it reopened the following year, Pasteur and two other administrators had been replaced. Pasteur was offered a teaching position at the Sorbonne, where he would not have to discipline rowdy students.

cultivated worms that hatched from eggs in nurseries were treated like newborn babies. The tiny silkworms ate mulberry leaves in huge quantities during what was called the "big gorge," and they shed their skins, or molted, four times before they were fully grown. At this point they spun pale gold, silky cocoons around themselves. Inside the cocoons the worms changed into pupae, or chrysalises, that developed into moths. After the moth broke out of the cocoons and mated, each female laid from six hundred to eight hundred eggs, and the cycle began again.

In the nurseries, Pasteur discovered, the breeders let some moths break out of their cocoons to produce eggs for the following season. The majority of cocoons, however, were put into a steam bath that killed the chrysalises. The breeders then harvested the silk that formed the cocoon by unwinding the threads, which could be dyed different colors and woven into shimmering silk cloth that was extremely light yet warm and durable.

The problem was that the sick silkworms were not spinning fully developed cocoons or were dying even before they

Workers wind silk off of cocoons. In 1865 Pasteur began investigating the epidemic responsible for decimating silkworm populations in southern France.

started to spin cocoons. Pasteur set up a field laboratory, started breeding silkworms, and began a systematic study of both healthy and blighted (sick) animals. It took many months to carry out the experiments since they had to be timed according to the life cycle of the silkworm. In addition, the work turned out to be complicated when Pasteur discovered that a second disease, called *flacherie* (flabby death), could also affect the worms. In the case of *flacherie*, the diseased worms became sluggish and then died.

A Personal Tragedy

Pasteur's work was interrupted by his own serious health problems. On the morning of October 19, 1868, he was scheduled to attend a session of the Academy of Sciences in Paris. Even though he did not feel well and had a tingling sensation down the left side of his body, Pasteur insisted on going to the meeting. Marie, who felt uneasy about his condition, went with him as far as the steps of the building. Pasteur stayed for the entire session and then walked home with Balard and another friend. After dinner, however, his symptoms grew worse; now he was not able to speak or move his left arm and leg. Pasteur had suffered a severe stroke, and his personal physician called in the famous Dr. Gabriel Andral of the Academy of Medicine.

At the time, doctors often treated many illnesses with bloodletting, on the theory that blood could somehow cause problems if it went "bad." Andral, there-

fore, prescribed the application of sixteen leeches behind the patient's ears. Pasteur's blood flowed freely, but that made little difference in his condition. Although he gradually recovered the ability to speak a little, Pasteur's family and many of his friends did not expect him to recover, and he himself thought he was dying. He told one friend, "I am sorry to die; I wanted to do much more for my country."[34]

For a week Pasteur was agitated, restless, and hardly able to sleep, but despite his pessimism, he began to make a slow recovery. His own doctor and friends, including Dumas, helped Marie nurse him. From morning till night visitors called to ask about his progress, and every morning the emperor and empress sent a servant to ask for news of his condition. Although he was physically helpless, Pasteur's mind was clear. The thought that he might not be able to finish his work on silkworm diseases disturbed him. One day he insisted on dictating to a friend a memorandum concerning an ingenious process he had discovered for detecting the eggs of silkworms that were predisposed to *flacherie*. When the members of the academy read this note, which was expressed in Pasteur's usual clear and concise language, they were greatly encouraged.

On November 30 Pasteur left his bed for the first time. From that date the doctors' daily bulletins reported his increasing activity: "(December 15): Progress slow but sure; he has walked from his bed to his armchair with some assistance. (December 22): he has gone into the

Fame and Honors

Louis Pasteur had no false modesty. He openly rejoiced in the honors and awards he received. He was delighted to be elected a member of the Paris Academy of Sciences in 1862, and he was gratified to receive the academy's Zecker Prize for his studies on fermentation and its Alhumbert Prize in natural science for his role in casting new light on the question of spontaneous generation. When he was awarded a grand prize at the World's Fair of 1867 for his work on wine-making fermentation, Pasteur reveled in the elaborate ceremony, which included a procession of the crowned heads of many European countries. The following year, in another grand ceremony, he was made a commander of the Legion of Honor. And the next year he was elected a fellow of the Royal Society of London.

Pasteur's growing reputation as a gifted scientist also earned him desirable teaching opportunities. His appointment as a professor at the School of Fine Arts in Paris was an honor that allowed Pasteur to make use of his talents as both an artist and a chemist. He taught his students how to perform simple experiments to reveal the properties of different pigments used in oil painting, and he showed them how architectural design influences human comfort and health. Pasteur's first lecture at the school was devoted to examining what he called the "important" question of sanitation and ventilation of hospitals, theaters, schools, meeting rooms, and private houses.

dining-room for dinner, leaning on a chair." And on December 29, two days after his forty-sixth birthday, "he has walked a few steps without support."[35]

His doctors advised a few months of convalescence, but Pasteur saw that as time wasted. It was more important, he insisted, to return to the work that might save many poor people from ruin than it was to be concerned about his personal health. As usual he had his way, and on January 18, three months after his stroke, Pasteur had himself transported to a train where a special compartment with a bed had been pre-

pared for him. Marie and their eleven-year-old daughter, Marie-Louise (Zizi), accompanied him.

Continuing Silkworm Studies

In the south of France the Pasteurs settled in a house near a silkworm nursery. At first, Pasteur spent his mornings in bed, where his three assistants came to him for their daily assignments. Marie or Zizi read the newspapers to him, and he dictated letters to Marie. After lunch, if the weather was nice, he moved out to the little garden, where his colleagues came to report to him on the day's work. After a quiet dinner with his wife and daughter, he was so exhausted he was ready to go to bed at 7:00 or 7:30. Pasteur kept hoping that he would regain the use of his left arm; however, it remained almost useless, and he continued to walk with a limp. He was forced to depend on his assistants for help in handling the scientific apparatuses used in carrying out the careful experiments he devised. Nevertheless, Pasteur plunged ahead eagerly with his work.

Now that he realized there were two different diseases involved, he could work out two different solutions for the silk-worm breeders. In *pebrine,* diseased moths transmitted the disease to their eggs, but the corpuscles, or microscopic cells, that indicated the disease were often visible only in adult moths. Therefore, Pasteur told the breeders, the solution was to have each moth lay her eggs on a separate piece of cloth. Then the breeders should dissect the moth and examine the tissues. If the tissues showed corpuscles, all of that moth's eggs should be destroyed; if there were no corpuscles in the tissues of the moth, her eggs should be allowed to produce worms, which should be healthy.

A silk farmer feeds mulberry leaves to silkworms. Pasteur studied the silkworm epidemic by conducting experiments at a local nursery.

The second disease affecting the industry called for a different solution. In *flacherie* the stomachs of the sick worms were full of gas and bacteria. Since the microorganisms responsible for the disease infected breeding chambers that were too crowded, too humid, or filled with moist mulberry leaves, Pasteur explained, it was necessary to keep the breeding chambers clean, well aired, and supplied with fresh leaves.

Pasteur had not found a cure for either disease, but he had discovered that both were contagious, and he was satisfied that he had established a dependable means of preventing infection to begin with. Still, there were those who refused to accept his conclusions. When challenges and criticisms of his work appeared in agricultural journals and newspapers, he was outraged, and Pasteur answered each critic with great indignation. Also, examining tissue or eggs under a microscope (or sending them off to be examined) was a baffling process to some of the breeders, who some-

Pasteur Answers His Critics

Not only did Pasteur have to deal with professional jealousy and with the prejudices of farmers who upheld the traditional practices of their ancestors, he also had to deal with the hostility of dealers in silkworm eggs who feared that Pasteur's methods threatened their financial security. Pasteur answered every letter and every article with facts and passion. René Dubos in Louis Pasteur *quotes a reply the eminent scientist wrote to one who questioned his results: "You do not know the first word of my investigations, of their results, of the principles which they have established, and of their practical implications. Most of them you have not read … and the others, you did not 'understand.'"*

The minister of agriculture asked Pasteur to submit a report on three lots of eggs that Mademoiselle Amat, a celebrated silkworm breeder, was distributing throughout the country. In his report, quoted in Louis Pasteur, *by René Dubos, Pasteur wrote:*

> Monsieur le Ministre, These three samples of seed are worthless. . . . They will in every instance succumb to corpuscle disease. If my seeding process had been employed, it would not have required ten minutes to discover that Mademoiselle Amat's cocoons, though excellent for spinning purposes, were absolutely unfit for reproduction. . . . For my part, I feel so sure of what I now affirm, that I shall not even trouble to test, by hatching them, the samples which you have sent me. I have thrown them into the river.

Pasteur's silkworm research was interrupted in 1868 when he suffered a stroke.

times did not follow Pasteur's directions correctly and then complained about the results. Dumas, Pasteur's faithful mentor, friend, and colleague, understood and sympathized with his frustration. "You have quacks to fight and envy to conquer, probably a hopeless task," he wrote. "The best [way] is to march right through them, Truth leading the way. It is not likely that they will be converted or reduced to silence."[36]

A Hectic Life

In Microbe Hunters, *Paul de Kruif vividly describes the frantic pace at which Pasteur drove himself (and everyone around him) when he was intent on solving a problem.*

He was everywhere around the tragic silk country, lecturing, asking innumerable questions, teaching the farmers to use microscopes, rushing back to the laboratory to direct his assistants—he directed them to do complicated experiments that he hadn't time to do, or even watch, himself—and in the evenings he dictated answers to letters and scientific papers and speeches to Madame Pasteur. The next morning he was off again to the neighboring towns, cheering up despairing farmers and haranguing them.

Throughout this period of his life, two of Pasteur's staunchest supporters were the emperor and empress of France. When Napoleon III offered him a place where he could continue to convalesce while he did further testing of his theories of silkworm diseases, Pasteur eagerly accepted. In November 1869 he, Marie, Zizi, and Jean-Baptiste moved to Villa Vicentina, the emperor's estate in Trieste (in what today is northern Italy), for a long stay. The two-story house was comfortable, and the grounds were beautiful, with spacious lawns and many trees. The family went for daily outings on foot or in a horse-drawn carriage.

Pasteur took the opportunity offered by this period of convalescence to encourage in his children the patriotic feelings his father had instilled in him. For Pasteur there was no greater example of a French patriot than Napoleon III's uncle, Napoleon Bonaparte, who had made France a world power that for a time ruled most of Europe. Pasteur wrote to a friend, "I am looking for all the works about Napoleon I in order to move my children's hearts by the great examples of glory and devotion."[37]

Even in this idyllic setting Pasteur's work, as always, came first. In addition to setting up hatcheries for silkworms, Pasteur began work on a book about the diseases of silkworms, which he dictated page by page to the patient Marie. There were many mulberry trees on this large estate, but for years *pebrine* and *flacherie* had ruined the silk industry in the area. Over the next nine months Pasteur was able to reestablish silk breeding on the estate and finished his book, *Studies on the Disease of the Silkworm*, which he dedicated to the empress Eugenie. In the dedication he thanked her for urging him to pursue his studies of the silkworm disease and for pointing out to him that, as he said, "Science is never grander than when it sets out to widen the scope of its beneficent applications." Pasteur added that he had endeavored to fulfill his promise to her by "five years of persevering research."[38] The book, which was published in 1870, would be used by Pasteur's laboratory workers and by other scientists as an introduction and guide to the study of infectious diseases in animals.

The five years he devoted to the study of the diseases affecting caterpillars had cost Pasteur dearly in time, energy, and health, but he had saved an important French industry. Perhaps even more importantly, what he learned through this research would lead him to significant discoveries in veterinary and human medicine.

Chapter Six

BATTLING INFECTIOUS DISEASES

In the years that followed his conquest of diseases threatening France's silk industry, Pasteur pursued the germ theory of disease. Neither vigorous opposition by other scientists nor his own physical handicaps slowed Pasteur's determination to discover the relationship between contagious diseases and the actions of those "infinitesimally small beings" he called microorganisms. Before Pasteur could embark on the major studies that would one day bring him worldwide renown and satisfy his desire to uncover some of life's greatest mysteries, a war intervened, stirring his passionate patriotism.

Surviving the Franco-Prussian War

On July 15, 1870, just after the Pasteurs had returned to Paris from Trieste, France declared war on Prussia, a large state in the German Empire. Soon other German states joined the conflict. The war was a disaster for France. After only a few weeks Napoleon III was forced to surrender to Prussia's William I. Humiliated by the defeat, the people of France demanded that the emperor turn power over to popularly elected leaders. The Second Empire was finished, but still the war continued. Soon, Paris was under siege.

The Pasteurs' son, Jean-Baptiste, had joined the army, but Pasteur himself, unable to enlist because of his physical condition, had remained in Paris. Now, as the advancing German army laid siege to the city, Pasteur took Marie and Zizi to Arbois. By leaving the city, the Pasteurs escaped the famine that accompanied the siege, during which starving Parisians ate dogs, cats, and even the animals in the zoo. Arbois, however, soon proved not to be the safe haven Pasteur had expected.

When German troops advanced on Arbois, Pasteur again retreated with his family to the south—just before shots rang out in the vineyards and enemy forces occupied the town. Pasteur felt bitterly humiliated when Paris surrendered after a four-month siege. He blamed the cata-strophe on the treachery and greed of Germany; what he called the inertia of Austria, Russia, and England; and the ignorance of the French military leaders. Above all, however, he blamed the defeat on the lack of foresight of French states-men in not supporting the sciences.

Perhaps he felt that with more empha-sis on the sciences France would have been

A contemporary illustration depicts starving Parisians waiting for food rations during the Franco-Prussian war. As the Germans invaded Paris, Pasteur and his family escaped to Arbois.

a stronger industrial and military nation, able to fight the war on an equal basis with the powerful Germans. In a letter to one of his students Pasteur wrote, "We are paying the penalty of fifty years' forgetfulness of science." The letter ended with a passionate outburst: "I wish that France may fight to her last man, to her last fortress. I wish that the war may be prolonged until the winter, when, the elements aiding us, all these Vandals may perish of cold and distress. Every one of my future works will bear on its title page the words: *Hatred to Prussia! Revenge! Revenge!*"[39] In 1868 the University of Bonn in Germany had conferred the honorary degree of doctor of medicine on Pasteur, and he had proudly accepted the honor. Now he sent the diploma back to the university, saying that the sight of it was odious to him.

In January, the Pasteurs became anxious about what might have happened to their son, from whom they had had no news in months. They set out in an old carriage to try to find the remnants of Jean-Baptiste's battalion. Traveling through heavy snowdrifts and pine forests, they finally found a soldier in the bedraggled, retreating force who told them that out of the twelve hundred men in their son's battalion only three hundred were left. Then they came across another soldier who told them that Sergeant Pasteur was alive but ill and pointed in the direction where they might find him. Happily they found Jean-Baptiste being transported in a cart and discovered that his illness had been caused mainly by fatigue and malnutrition. After

a few weeks of recovery, Jean-Baptiste rejoined his regiment and remained with it until France capitulated and the Treaty of Frankfurt was signed in May 1871.

The Beer of Revenge

The war had resulted in France's humiliation, but this did not change Pasteur's feelings about his native land. Indeed, his next major project was influenced by his intense patriotism. He hated the fact that Germany was superior to France in any way, and beyond question the Germans were superior in the manufacture of beer. Pasteur had begun an intensive study of the brewing process while he was in exile from Paris during the war. Now, he decided to see if he could find a way to make French beer competitive with that of Germany.

In April 1871, Pasteur moved his family to Clermont-Ferrand, in south central France. After settling Marie and Zizi into a few rooms in the home of a former student, Émile Duclaux, he set up a makeshift laboratory in a corner of the chemistry laboratory of the Faculty of Sciences school. Then he began visiting the nearby Kuhn brewery. Although he was a skillful brewer, the owner, M. Kuhn, did not know much about what actually happened during the brewing process. All he knew was how to carry out the complicated process, mixing malted barley and hops in the right quantities and adding yeast to create his product. Kuhn's quality-control method (like that of other brewers) was to throw away the yeast he was using and replace it

Pasteur monitors the enormous vat he designed to kill harmful bacteria during the beer fermentation process. His research on brewing techniques revolutionized the beer industry.

with fresh yeast whenever customers in cafés began complaining about the taste of the beer. He told Pasteur that in hot weather, the beer was likely to become acid or moldy, and that sometimes the fermented beer seemed to spoil for no reason.

The work that Pasteur did in solving the problems of the beer industry was an extension of the research he had done on the fermentation of wine. He demonstrated that the changes in beer were caused by microscopic organisms, and showed the beer makers ways of eliminating them. He also invented a technique for pasteurizing beer that eliminated the need for continuous refrigeration, saving the brewers a great deal of money.

Pasteur continued his studies on beer for several years, visiting other breweries in France and traveling to England to study the vast beer-making industry there. To his chagrin, the practical English brewers were even quicker to adopt his suggestions for maintaining the quality of their beer than were the French brewers, although the latter, too, eventually adopted his suggestions. Pasteur took out several patents on his improved beer-making techniques and wrote a book called *Studies on Beer*, which was published in 1876. With his permission, the book was soon translated into English, but he refused all requests to translate it into German. He called his improved product "the beer of revenge" and had no intention of giving the hated Germans easy access to his discoveries.

The Germ Theory of Disease

Even while he was involved in studying the relationship between microorganisms and problems in the beer industry, Pasteur began an intensive campaign to promote the theory that living organisms cause disease. In 1873–1874 he began an arduous round of visits to hospitals, which many

Germ Phobia

In a paper read before the French Academy of Sciences in April 1878 titled "The Germ Theory and Its Applications to Medicine and Surgery," Pasteur told the assembled dignitaries that germs abound on the surfaces of all objects and said, "If it is a terrifying thought that life is at the mercy of the multiplication of these minute bodies, it is a consoling hope that Science will not always remain powerless before such enemies." In the meantime, Pasteur demonstrated his deep belief in the dangers of infection from germs by avoiding shaking hands as much as possible. He also wiped his glassware and dinnerware carefully at meals, and to the surprise and sometimes dismay of his hostesses, he closely inspected bread that was served to him, putting aside any little speck he found in it.

people at that time considered pestholes—a place to go only when they were ready to die. Pasteur repeatedly pointed out that the majority of people there died not from their original complaints but from infections they developed in the hospitals. During the Franco-Prussian War, for example, out of the thirteen thousand soldiers undergoing operations, ten thousand died—not from their wounds but from infection.

Many physicians, however, considered this germ theory of disease to be nonsense. Instead, these doctors insisted that diseases and infections were caused by miasmas (unhealthy vapors in the air), inherited tendencies, poor nutrition, alcoholism, and other personal traits that made the patient susceptible. They ridiculed Pasteur as a mere chemist who had never studied medicine. Ignoring his detractors, Pasteur continued his efforts to make doctors realize they should not only try to cure disease but try to prevent it. Pasteur demanded that doctors wash their hands before they touched their patients and that surgeons sterilize their instruments before operating. Doggedly stalking through hospital sickrooms, he took hundreds of samples and spent hundreds of hours examining them under his microscope, trying to pinpoint the specific microbes that caused certain infections.

In addition to the large numbers of deaths resulting from infections following operations in hospitals, an immense number of deaths occurred in maternity wards where young mothers died from puerperal, or "childbed," fever. In March 1879 Pasteur attended a discussion on the caus-es of puerperal fever at the Academy of Medicine.

After listening for some time to a doctor expounding on the causes of infection in women after their babies had been delivered, Pasteur interrupted the speaker, saying, "None of those things cause the epidemic; it is the nursing and medical staff who carry the microbe from an infected woman to a healthy one." When the orator said he was afraid that such a microbe could never be found, Pasteur went to the blackboard and drew a diagram of organisms shaped like strings of beads. "There, that is what it is like!"[40] he told the doctors. What he had drawn was a picture of the microorganism (now well known as streptococcus) that he had found in the blood clots and organs of women who suffered from childbed fever.

Although some doctors still stubbornly refused to accept the germ theory, there were an increasing number who appreciated Pasteur's work and welcomed his suggestions. Among these was Joseph Lister, a brilliant English surgeon. Lister had kept up with Pasteur's work since his earliest writings on the role of microbes, or bacteria, in fermentation. He had also read Pasteur's descriptions of his experiments to debunk the theory of spontaneous generation.

Lister had taken to heart his French colleague's theories about the great harm microscopic creatures might cause. Realizing that germs could enter a wound during surgery, Lister sterilized all his instruments, sponges, and bandages in carbolic acid, and he and his assistants washed their hands in a solution of it. While they operated, a vaporizer sprayed an antiseptic mist of carbolic acid over the wound. The results were dramatic. Deaths of patients operated on using this procedure dropped from 50 percent to between 2 and 3 percent.

In February 1874, Lister wrote to Pasteur thanking him for his "brilliant researches," which he said had demonstrated "the truth of the germ theory of putrefaction, and thus furnished me with the principle upon which alone the antiseptic system can be carried out." Lister invited Pasteur to come to visit his hospital so he could see "how largely mankind is being benefited by your labours." [41] Pasteur was gratified by Lister's praise and by that of other respected physicians; however, his search for microbes that cause infections and diseases continued—not in humans, but in sheep.

Joseph Lister (center) prepares to operate as carbolic mist is sprayed over his patient's wound. This and other disinfecting procedures greatly reduced the death rate of patients.

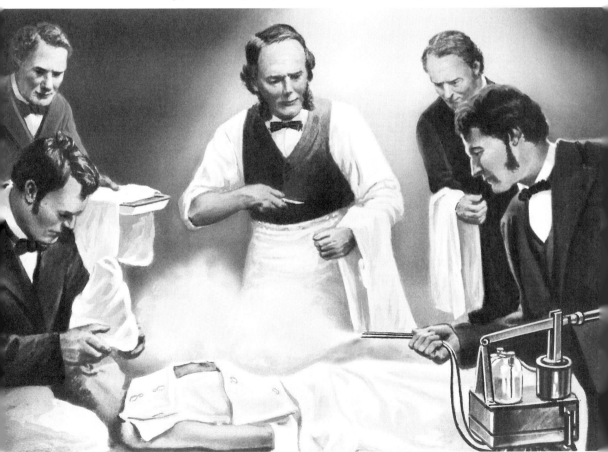

Antisepsis and Asepsis

Antisepsis destroys microbes; *asepsis* prevents them. Long before the germ theory of disease was established by Pasteur in the nineteenth century, antisepsis (preventing infection by killing or inhibiting the growth of microorganisms) was attempted in ancient times by the use of such disinfectants as wine, boiling oil, or vinegar. More recently, before there were antibiotics, iodine, carbolic acid, or silver sulfate was used as an antiseptic. Lister used carbolic acid during surgery because it had been proved effective in purifying sewage.

A kind of asepsis (the means employed to prevent contamination by infectious agents) was used in the nineteenth century by medical personnel like Florence Nightingale, who insisted on a clean environment for patients even though she did not accept the germ theory of disease. It was several decades after Pasteur's discoveries of the danger of contamination by microbes that the use of sterilized dressings and instruments and the wearing of sterile gloves and gowns during surgical and obstetrical procedures became routine in hospitals.

Anthrax: A Deadly Killer

By the late 1870s a serious disease was ruining the livestock industry throughout Europe. Animals, especially sheep and cows, infected with this disease, known as anthrax, became sick and died suddenly. One day the animals seemed healthy, the next they trembled, gasped for breath, and keeled over in pools of blood. People who worked with these domestic animals, including farmers, shepherds, butchers, and sheep shearers, frequently experienced sore areas on their bodies, fever, blood poisoning, and pneumonia in some cases, and some died. Furthermore, even if a farmer removed a dead animal, healthy animals grazing in an affected pasture could sicken and die much later on.

For several decades European scientists had tried to discover the cause of this deadly disease. In 1876 a young German physician, Robert Koch, published a major paper on anthrax. Working in a primitive laboratory in his home, Koch had discovered that when the anthrax bacteria were dried out, they formed spores, which consisted of dormant bacteria protected by a tough outer shell. These spores, he discovered, could survive for a long time, and the bacteria could come back to life years later. This was the reason the disease persisted in certain locations. Koch had also reported that the germs responsible for anthrax could be grown in the laboratory.

When Pasteur decided to tackle the problem of anthrax in February 1877, he had Koch's conclusions available, as well as those of other scientists who had studied the disease, but as always with his research, he began by confirming previous findings for himself.

Solving Some of the Mysteries of Anthrax

Pasteur's first task was to prove that the rod-shaped anthrax bacteria were in fact responsible for the animals' symptoms, something many scientists rejected. To begin double-checking the results of other researchers, Pasteur inserted a drop of blood full of the tiny rods into a flask filled with two ounces of a nutrient solution. When the rods began to multiply, he removed a single drop of the liquid and put it into a second flask filled with nutrient. After he had repeated this procedure one hundred times, he was left with an extremely diluted blood solution. If, as other scientists said, some chemical in the blood killed the animals, that chemical should now be so diluted as to be harmless. Yet, when Pasteur injected liquid from the one hundredth flask into several rabbits and guinea pigs, all the animals died.

Despite the fact that the blood was greatly diluted, the bacteria had flourished. Pasteur had proved that the rods

Pasteur as Observer

Many of Pasteur's contemporaries commented on his ability to concentrate on a problem to the point of losing awareness of place and time. Pasteur's son-in-law, René Vallery-Radot, in his biography of the great scientist, tells of one such incident at a farm where the sheep were infected with anthrax.

[When they reached the farm] Pasteur hurried to the folds. Standing motionless by the gate, he would gaze at the lots which were being experimented upon, with a careful attention which nothing escaped; he would spend hours watching one sheep which seemed to him to be sickening. We had to remind him of the time and to point out to him that the towers of Chartres Cathedral were beginning to disappear in the falling darkness before we could prevail upon him to come away. He questioned farmers and their servants, giving much credit to the opinions of shepherds, who on account of their solitary life, give their whole attention to their flocks and often become sagacious [knowledgeable] observers.

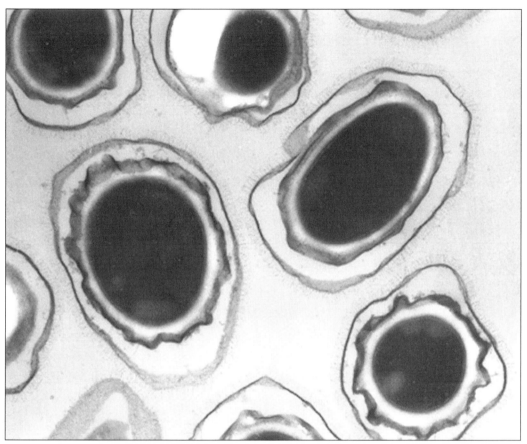

Pasteur discovered that the tiny spores (pictured) produced by the anthrax bacteria could survive and remain infectious for years.

were the killers, but he still needed to discover where the anthrax bacteria came from and why seemingly perfectly healthy animals suddenly fell ill with anthrax and died. One day as he was watching sheep graze in a field Pasteur noticed that the earth was a different color in one part of the field. The farmer explained that that was where he had buried several sheep that died of anthrax. Pasteur also noticed a number of tiny mounds made by earthworms. Immediately it occurred to him

that they might be the answer to the mystery.

Back in the laboratory, Pasteur extracted earth from the intestine of one of the earthworms and injected it into guinea pigs, which promptly developed anthrax. He had solved another one of the mysteries connected with anthrax. Although anthrax germs were delicate and died when exposed to air, the tiny spores they produced were tough and could survive for years. When a grazing animal ingested them in the pastures churned up by earthworms, the bacteria began to multiply, and the animal came down with anthrax. Pasteur quickly advised farmers not to bury animals that died of anthrax in their fields but to burn the bodies or bury them in sandy or chalky soils where there were no earthworms.

This advice helped the farmers who heeded it, but Pasteur was far from satisfied. He wanted to discover the means of preventing anthrax altogether—*and* to discover how to prevent other contagious diseases in humans as well as in animals. The answers to those mysteries were still many experiments away.

Chapter Seven

CREATING VACCINES TO FIGHT DISEASES

Pasteur continued his work on contagious diseases in animals with the goal of developing vaccines to prevent these diseases. One of the vaccines he would develop would protect animals and humans from rabies. This victory would bring much fame, but the creation of vaccines for sheep anthrax and chicken cholera and other devastating contagious animal diseases would also prove to be of great benefit to people throughout the world.

Family Life vs. Career

Without the help of an excellent team of assistants, Pasteur would not have been able to accomplish all that he did in the last two decades of his life. The team included Émile Duclaux, a chemist, and Émile Roux, a physician, whose medical training was a great asset. Pasteur was not an easy taskmaster, but he drove himself even harder than he did his assistants.

Although Pasteur cherished his wife and children, his schedule left little time for family life. He was in the laboratory by 8:30 every morning, where he worked for three hours before taking time out for lunch with Marie. On most afternoons he attended meetings at the academies of science or medicine, where he often heard theories expounded that roused him to fury—and sometimes to ferocious debate. His friends tried in vain to keep him from expending energy by responding to men who were not in the same class with him as scientists. Balard urged restraint and Duclaux wrote to him affectionately, "I can see very well what you stand to lose in these fights: your peace of mind, your time, your health. I fail to see what you can gain by them."[42] After the meetings,

Pasteur would return to the peace and quiet of his laboratory and work until late afternoon when he dictated his notes to Marie.

Each summer Pasteur would return to Arbois and the family homestead, which he now owned. Here he remained

Pasteur spent time with his grandchildren (pictured is his granddaughter) when his schedule permitted.

until midautumn, following much the same work schedule as he had in Paris, except there were no meetings to attend. Aside from field trips, he spent most of his time in the laboratory he had created in Arbois. On Sundays he would accompany Marie to hear mass at the church of Saint-Just, and afterward they would have his sister Virginie and her family over for dinner. Pasteur spent little time on recreational activities, but he did enjoy brief games of croquet, short walks (when Marie could entice him out), and on rainy days a round of billiards.

Pasteur worried about his son, who had failed in his attempt to earn a law degree and showed little ambition in any other direction. When Jean-Baptiste married in 1875, Pasteur wrote to his son's mother-in-law advising her not to live with the couple, who, he said, needed time to be together without a third party present. He advised his son to make his wife his ally but not to be governed by her.

Pasteur was much more enthusiastic about the marriage of his daughter, Marie-Louise, in 1879. He had great admiration for his new son-in-law, René Vallery-Radot, who was secretary to the minister of public works and a promising young journalist. Like Pasteur, Vallery-Radot was almost fanatically patriotic, and the two got along splendidly. Eventually the couple presented Pasteur with a granddaughter and a grandson in whom he delighted.

Pasteur developed a vaccine that eradicated the cholera strain that decimated populations of farm fowl.

With her children now married, Marie carried on as the best ally of her work-obsessed husband. During the days she patiently copied out in her neat handwriting the lengthy articles he dictated to her, and in the evenings she read the newspapers to her husband and took more dictation. On their thirty-fifth wedding anniversary she wrote to Zizi: "Your father, very busy as always, says little to me, sleeps little, and gets up at dawn—in a word, continues the life that I began with him thirty-five years ago today."[43]

Chicken Cholera

One of the problems that absorbed Pasteur's attention was a disease that raged among fowl on farms in France. It was called chicken cholera (although it was not related to human cholera). When chicken cholera struck a barnyard, it spread rapidly, killing most of the birds within a day or two. The Pasteur team began their study of chicken cholera the same way they had approached anthrax, by isolating the bacterium that caused the disease; then they cultivated the germs in the laboratory in flasks filled with a growth medium. When healthy hens were injected with the fresh culture, they quickly died. The team knew how to give the chickens cholera, but they were unable to make recommendations to farmers on how to protect their fowl.

Then a lucky break led the way to an important discovery. When hens were injected with a batch of chicken cholera bacteria that had been kept in the laboratory over the summer (while Pasteur was away in Arbois), they did not come down with the disease. Pasteur immediately devised a series of experiments to uncover the meaning of this development.

A new, virulent culture was made up and injected into an untreated batch of chickens and also into the chickens that had survived inoculation with the old batch of culture. The newly injected chickens all died, but almost all of the previously inoculated hens survived. Again, Pasteur's prepared mind allowed him to realize the potential significance of an accidental occurrence.

Pasteur was already aware that with certain diseases one attack conferred immunity against another attack of the same disease. For example, this is true of measles or rubella. Pasteur also knew that immunity to one disease, smallpox, could be imparted by vaccination. Thinking that injection with the old batch of chicken cholera had in a similar way provided immunity to that disease, he set out to develop a vaccine.

Working through a series of experiments, Pasteur and his team found that exposing the chicken cholera bacteria to oxygen attenuated, or weakened, them. After further experiments, they came up with just the right vaccine culture—one weak enough to give the chickens a mild case of the disease without killing them, but strong enough to provide immunity in the event of later exposure to the disease. In the summer of 1880 Pasteur announced the successful preparation of his vaccine.

Now he was eager to apply what he had learned about immunity to discovering a vaccine for anthrax. It would not be as easy as he hoped. Pasteur and his team found that oxygen attenuation of anthrax germs was unreliable. So they had to find a different method of growing weakened strains of anthrax bacteria. Roux heard of a method of attenuation using antiseptic compounds such as carbolic acid. The Pasteur team tried the antiseptic attenuation technique and found it worked.

The Great Anthrax Trial

When Pasteur announced that his laboratory had found a way to produce a vaccine to protect sheep against the dreaded anthrax, there were many skeptics. Almost immediately he was challenged to prove in a public demonstration that he could prevent anthrax. Pasteur accepted the challenge, to the dismay of his assistants and friends, who believed that much more work was needed on the vaccine before it was ready to be tested publicly. Only fourteen sheep had been successfully treated in the laboratory, whereas the trial Pasteur had agreed to involved fifty animals. The exhibition was to be held at Pouilly le Fort, a small village not far from Paris.

The flock of fifty sheep was divided in two. Twenty-five were to be vaccinated and then given an injection of full-strength anthrax germs. The other half would not be vaccinated but would be given the same dose of full-strength germs. The vaccine was given in two injections, on May 5 and May 17, 1881. Then on May 31 all of the sheep received injections of fresh, virulent anthrax germs. When some of the vaccinated sheep became feverish the next day, Pasteur was in despair. If the trial failed, his reputation would be ruined. He knew that many veterinarians and physicians hoped that the occasion would be the downfall of his germ theory of disease and that he would be heaped with scorn.

The next day there was good news, and his spirits rose: All of the vaccinated sheep were well. On the other hand, eighteen of the unprotected sheep were dead, and the others were dying. The field trial had been well publicized, and when Pasteur and his

Edward Jenner and Vaccination

Smallpox has always been one of the most dreaded diseases. It is also one of the most contagious of all diseases, and in ancient times, crude forms of vaccination were practiced. In China, small pieces of the crusts of smallpox pustules were placed into the nostrils of a healthy person. In Africa, healers rubbed pus from a sore of a person with a mild case of smallpox into a scratch on the skin of a healthy person. Early in the eighteenth century, smallpox inoculation became fashionable at the English court when Lady Mary Montagu introduced a method she had learned in Turkey. Pus taken from a smallpox victim was preserved in a nutshell and then transferred to the patient by pricking him or her with the tip of a needle that had been dipped in the pus.

The English physician Edward Jenner came up with a better idea. He began a series of experiments in 1796 that eventually led to the development of a vaccine against the dreaded disease. Jenner died the year after Pasteur was born, but Pasteur was well aware of his predecessor's accomplishments. When he used the term *vaccinate,* Pasteur acknowledged the origin of the term in a speech he gave in London in 1881. Biographer Patrice Debré, in *Louis Pasteur,* reproduces Pasteur's remarks: "I have given to the term *vaccination* an extension which science, I hope, will adopt as an homage to the merits and the immense services rendered by one of the greatest men England has produced, your own Jenner."

assistants arrived at Pouilly le Fort on June 2, they found a huge crowd gathered to witness the results of the trial. By the end of the day, all of the unprotected sheep had died, and all of the vaccinated sheep were well. The crowd showered praise and acclaim on Pasteur, who stood up in his carriage and exclaimed triumphantly to the detractors who had come hoping to see him fail, "Well, then! Men of little faith!"[44]

The successful trial made converts out of those veterinarians who had doubted Pasteur, and soon his laboratory was mak-

A doctor in New Guinea administers the anthrax vaccine to sheep in the early 1900s. Veterinarians around the world began to use Pasteur's vaccine shortly after he introduced it in 1881.

ing and selling the vaccine in large quantities. Less than a decade later, millions of animals had been spared anthrax through vaccination. The government of France recognized Pasteur by raising his salary from twelve thousand to twenty-five thousand francs a year. In addition, he was awarded the Grand Cross, the highest rank in the Legion of Honor, and at Pasteur's request two of his collaborators, Émile Roux and Charles Chamberland, were made knights in the legion.

One immediate reward of this daring public test was Pasteur's election as a member of the Academie Française, the most prestigious scholarly body in France. The forty members, all of them men, were referred to as "immortals" by the press and by the public in recognition of their lasting contributions to their fields. The director of the Academie welcomed Pasteur, who attended the inaugural ceremony wearing a green and gold frock coat. "Your scientific work is like a luminous ray in the vast night of the infinitely small, in those utmost depths of being where life is born," the director told him. "Take your place with the elite who assure themselves against nothingness by a single method: creating works that last." [45]

Chapter Eight

THE FINAL VICTORY

Pasteur's determination to conquer disease led him to what would be hailed as his greatest achievement, the development of an antirabies vaccine for animals and humans. This final victory over disease made Pasteur an international hero. He was called a savior by people all over the world. Yet developing this vaccine proved to be an arduous and sometimes dangerous process.

Hunting Killer Germs

Following his success in preventing anthrax, Pasteur undertook several other projects involving diseases that afflicted domestic animals. One of his most important studies had to do with a disease that was killing pigs in large numbers. It was called swine erysipelas, or *rouget* (the "red disease"). Animals affected developed a fever, broke out in red or purple blotches,

and quickly died. In 1879 *rouget* had killed over 1 million pigs in the United States, and in the early 1880s it raged in England and Germany as well as in France.

Pasteur was soon in hot pursuit of the microbe that caused the disease and bent on finding a vaccine to prevent it. Traveling with his team of collaborators, he visited different pig farms where the disease was devastating the herds. He wrote to Marie, telling her: "There are sick swine everywhere, some dying, some dead. . . . This reminds me of the *pebrine,* with pigsties and sick pigs instead of nurseries full of dying silkworms. Not ten thousand, but at least twenty thousand swine have perished." [46] After many painstaking experiments, the Pasteur team did develop an effective vaccination, which was a great boon to pork-producing countries.

Trial and Error

As important as Pasteur knew his work on chicken cholera, anthrax, and *rouget* had been, he believed that what he had learned about the preparation of vaccines might be put to even greater use, battling one of the most dreaded of all communicable diseases—rabies. The disease called rabies, or hydrophobia, is named for the symptoms it causes. *Rabies* is from the Latin meaning rage or fury; *hydrophobia* is from the Greek meaning "fear of water." In terms of numbers of human victims, rabies was not a major killer. Still, although relatively

Pasteur studies laboratory animals he has inoculated with the rabies vaccine. Pasteur worked with dozens of different animals to devise a potent vaccine against the disease.

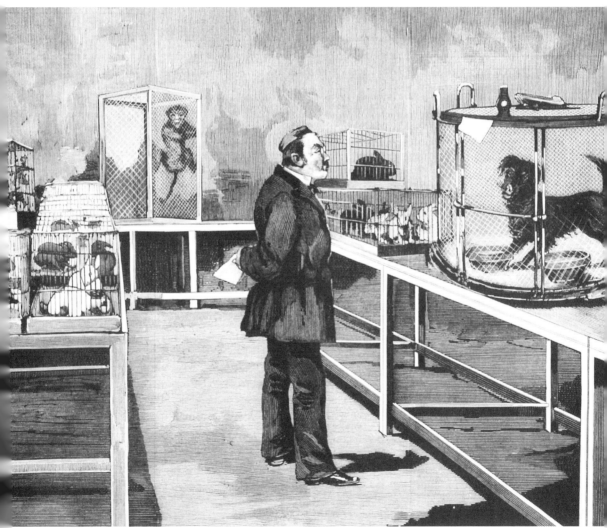

few people died in any given year from the disease, rabies was a source of mystery and horror. Animals afflicted with the disease were aggressive, attacking other animals and humans without provocation.

Not everyone bitten by a rabid animal developed rabies, but once symptoms appeared, death was almost inevitable. How one was affected varied from one individual to the next, but usually the first symptom was pain or numbness at the site of the infection. This was followed by severe headache and restlessness. Swallowing and breathing became difficult, and although the craving for water was intense, victims were unable to drink because of muscle spasms in their throats. Later, patients might suffer violent convulsions before falling into a coma and dying.

The methods for preventing rabies—cauterizing the wound by searing it with a caustic acid or red-hot iron—were almost as horrific as the disease itself. Pasteur had vivid memories from his childhood of the rabid wolf that rampaged through his hometown, biting men and beasts, and of the screams of the victims when the village blacksmith had applied a red-hot poker to their wounds.

For their research on rabies, Pasteur and his chief collaborator, Émile Roux, had to develop new methods of experimentation. At first they tried to find a rabies microbe as they had done for other

Taking Risks

The first two mad dogs brought to Pasteur's laboratory were given to him by M. Bourrel, an old army veterinary surgeon. In trying to find a remedy for rabies, Bourrel had come up with the preventative measure of filing down the teeth of dogs so that they could not puncture the skin if they bit. The veterinarian hoped that Pasteur could develop a vaccine against the disease and agreed to send him a telegram whenever one of the dogs in his kennels developed symptoms of rabies. Pasteur's son-in-law, René Vallery-Radot, in The Life of Pasteur, *described the risks Pasteur, and those working with him, took in performing the experiments.*

One day, Pasteur having wished to collect a little saliva from the jaws of a rabid dog, so as to obtain it directly, two of Bourrel's assistants undertook to drag a mad bulldog, foaming at the mouth, from its cage; they seized it by means of a lasso, and stretched it on a table. These two men, thus associated with Pasteur in the same danger, with the same calm heroism, held the struggling, ferocious animal down with their powerful hands, whilst the scientist drew, by means of a glass tube held between his lips, a few drops of the deadly saliva.

diseases, but when they examined blood and tissue samples under their microscopes, they could not see a bacterium that might cause the disease. The reason, although Pasteur had no way of knowing this, was that the disease is caused not by a bacterium but by a virus, a particle too small to detect with the microscopes in use at that time. Still, Pasteur and his team were sure some infectious agent was present. Unable to see a microbe, the team found that the technique of growing a culture in flasks also would not work. The team concluded that they would have to culture the rabies organism in animal bodies.

Culturing the rabies organism in an animal presented another problem, which was the lengthy incubation period that occurred before a healthy animal actually came down with rabies. Injecting healthy animals with saliva drawn from rabid animals shortened the wait, but this was a tricky and dangerous procedure. Still, Pasteur performed it many times. Finally, realizing that the disease primarily affected the nervous system, the team made extracts from spinal cords of rabid animals and injected those directly into the brains of dogs that had been anesthetized. With this technique they could predictably produce rabies in the test animals in a few days.

Now their goal was to find a technique for producing a vaccine that could be given to the victim of a bite from a rabid animal and prevent rabies from developing. They tried injecting dogs with different amounts of preparations made from saliva, blood, and the ground-up brains of rabid rabbits, but the results were unreliable and unpredictable. Sometimes the test subjects got rabies; sometimes they did not. The team performed a series of experiments, transmitting the disease up to ninety times in guinea pigs, rabbits, and monkeys—still with uneven results.

Then Roux came up with an ingenious approach. A strip of spinal cord from a rabid rabbit was suspended in the center of a bottle, which had a hole in the top and one on the lower side. Air entered from the bottom opening, passed over a drying agent, and exited from the top. The longer the cord dried, the less potent the infectious agent in the tissue became. An extract made by mincing the driest cord was injected under the skin of a dog. This injection was followed every day for the next twelve days with extracts of increasing potency. At the end of that time, the vaccinated dogs proved to be completely resistant to infection. The success of these experiments was extremely gratifying, but the ultimate proof—testing the vaccine on humans—was yet to come. As word of his research on rabies leaked out, Pasteur began receiving entreaties to help people who had been bitten by rabid animals. He began to do so reluctantly, treating two victims of bites from rabid animals. Unfortunately, one of his patients was already in the late stages of the disease and was therefore beyond help. The other patient received a single dose of the

Because Pasteur was unable to observe the virus responsible for rabies, he knew that the traditional method of growing cultures in flasks would not work.

vaccine, but then was sent home after the hospital's director refused to allow further treatment. Pasteur was never allowed further contact with the patient and therefore never learned whether his treatment worked.

Joseph Meister

The first opportunity to really test his vaccine came on July 6, 1885, when Joseph Meister, the nine-year-old son of a baker, was brought to Pasteur. A quick examination convinced Pasteur that the boy, with fourteen serious bite wounds, was definitely at risk of developing rabies. Pasteur wrote in his notebook, "Severely bitten on the middle finger of the right hand, on the thighs, and on the leg by the same rabid dog that tore his trousers, threw him down and would have devoured him if it had not been for the arrival of a mason armed with two iron bars who beat down the dog."[47]

Pasteur was torn as to whether to treat the boy in his laboratory or send him to a hospital and treat him there. If he treated him privately, he would be able to administer and monitor the treatments without fear of interference by hospital staff. On the other hand, if he did that and the boy did not survive, Pasteur's reputation was on the line, and he might be subject to legal action. Roux was opposed to treating the boy, but Pasteur consulted two well-respected doctors, who were also his personal friends.

After examining Joseph, the physicians, who were familiar with Pasteur's research, advised him to administer the antirabies treatment. If nothing was done, they agreed, the boy was doomed to a horrible death. Joseph and his mother were given a comfortable room, in an annex to the laboratory, and the first injection was administered on July 6 with the oldest and weakest spinal cord extract. Over the next ten days, Joseph was inoculated twelve times, each time with an increasingly virulent dose of vaccine. As he became used to his surroundings, he enjoyed playing with the laboratory mice

and guinea pigs, and he became increasingly fond of "Dear Monsieur Pasteur." Joseph ate and slept well, but Pasteur did not.

Pasteur became increasingly tense as the treatment progressed. He alternated between hopes and fears and suffered from nightmares of what might happen

Pasteur observes as Joseph Meister is injected with the rabies vaccine. The vaccination was a success.

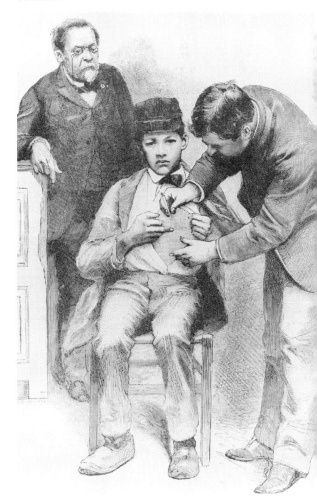

after the last and most potent inoculation. Marie wrote to her daughter, "This will be another bad night for your father. He cannot come to terms with the idea of applying a measure of last resort to this child. And yet he now has to go through with it. The little fellow continues to feel very well." [48] Fortunately, Joseph Meister continued in good health. When he returned home, he wrote frequently to Pasteur as he had promised to do. Pasteur wrote back, sending the boy a picture of himself and postage stamps for his letters.

Another challenge Pasteur faced came in the fall of 1885, when he returned to Paris after spending his usual working vacation in Arbois. The victim this time was a fifteen-year-old shepherd, Jean-Baptiste Jupille, who had been severely bitten as he struggled to keep a rabid dog away from his fellow shepherds. Touched by the story of the boy's bravery, Pasteur agreed to treat him in the same way he had treated Joseph Meister. The problem was, Pasteur explained, that Jupille's bites would already be six days old when the treat-

Russian Victims

In March 1886, among those flocking to Pasteur's laboratory for rabies treatments were nineteen Russians. A rabid wolf had left them with terrible wounds. A priest had had his upper lip and right cheek torn off by a surprise attack as he was entering his church. The youngest in the group had had the skin of his forehead torn off by the teeth of the wolf, and others had suffered similar serious bites. A Russian doctor, who accompanied the group, told Pasteur how the wolf had terrified the area for two days and two nights until one of its victims struck the wolf down with an ax.

Five of the Russians had such serious wounds that they were immediately taken to the hospital. Pasteur decided that since two weeks had passed between the time of their bites and their arrival at the laboratory, all of the victims should receive two inoculations a day. The patients in the hospital received their injections there; the other fourteen Russians came every morning and every evening to the laboratory to have their wounds treated and receive their injections. With their thick beards and fur coats, they lined up with the other patients. The only French word they knew was "Pasteur." It was too late to save three of the Russian victims, but the other sixteen survived and went home to sing Pasteur's praises. The Russian czar sent his brother to France to give to Pasteur the Cross of the Order of St. Anne of Russia in diamonds. He also sent one hundred thousand francs for the fund being collected to build the Pasteur Institute.

ments began, whereas Joseph Meister's were only sixty hours old when his treatment began. Pasteur did not know how long a period could elapse between the attack and the start of injections for them to be effective. Again, however, the outcome was a complete success, and Jupille returned home cured.

The Pasteur Institute

As word spread that Pasteur had developed a vaccine that would prevent rabies, victims of dog and wolf bites streamed into his laboratory. Every morning at 11 o'clock patients lined up to receive injections, and everywhere people eagerly followed the accounts of these treatments in newspapers and magazines. The president of the Academy of Sciences declared that Pasteur had achieved "one of the greatest advances that has ever been accomplished in medicine."[49] Pasteur found that he had become a hero and a legend.

Nevertheless, some failures did occur when the time between a bite and the start of the treatment was too long. Pasteur therefore continued to work to perfect the vaccine and the technique of administering it. He described the treatment as a race: "Rabies, with its relatively slow incubation period, is like a local train; the vaccine overtakes it like an express train, and after having overtaken it, keeps it from entering into the body."[50]

When the clinic Pasteur had set up in his laboratory became overwhelmed by the staggering number of victims that continued to arrive, he suggested that a larger

As word of Pasteur's successful rabies treatment spread, patients like these children bitten by a rabid dog lined up for injections.

independent facility was needed. The response from a grateful public was immediate and generous. The new clinic, which was known as the Pasteur Institute, was funded by charitable contributions that arrived from all over the world. In addition to being a center for rabies treatment, it was set up for research on other infectious diseases and also for teaching. Émile Duclaux, Pasteur's former student, oversaw the planning of what newspapers dubbed the "Rabies Palace" on a large vacant lot on the southwest edge of Paris.

The Last Years

Pasteur watched the progress of this capstone of his career with intense pride and

Pasteur's Philosophy

As Pasteur's life drew gently to a close, his body grew weaker, but his mind remained as alert and curious as ever. In the new garden at the Pasteur Institute, a little tent was set up for him. Here he sat in his black skullcap, watching the comings and goings of the workers at the institute and visiting with colleagues and friends. His faithful friend of fifty years, Charles Chappuis, now honorary rector of the Academy of Dijon, came often to sit with him and talk of philosophical and spiritual matters.

Early in his career, Pasteur had declared that experimental science did not concern itself with the origin of the world or its final destiny. Biographer Patrice Debré, in *Louis Pasteur,* quotes his subject as saying, "The notion of the supernatural is embedded in every heart." God is a "form of the idea of the infinite," he said, "whether the God is called Brahma, Allah, Jehovah or Jesus." And Pasteur asked, "Where are the true sources of human dignity, of liberty and modern democracy, if not in the notion of the infinite before which all men are equal."

interest. His health, however, was failing. In October 1887, Pasteur suffered a second stroke. After a time he regained his ability to speak, but his words were weak and slurred, and he had more difficulty walking. He attended the grand ceremony that marked the opening of the Pasteur Institute on November 14, 1888, leaning on the arm of his son. Among those attending were the president of France, ambassadors from many countries, and numerous prominent scientists. In Pasteur's remarks, which were read to the audience by his son, he said that he regretted having to appear before them as a man "vanquished by time." He urged his collaborators and students to keep up their enthusiasm, but warned them to "let it ever be regulated by rigorous examina-tions and tests. Never advance anything which cannot be proved in a simple and decisive fashion." He promised them that "When, after so many efforts, you have at last arrived at a certainty, your joy is one of the greatest which can be felt by a human soul."[51]

As he became more plagued by fatigue and illness and less able to spend time in the laboratory, Pasteur relied more on his family for solace. He and Marie moved into comfortable quarters in an annex to the institute, where she helped him keep up with his voluminous correspondence. Marie-Louise and René visited every day, and Pasteur was a doting grandfather to their children, Camille and Louis. His son Jean-Baptiste and his wife, Jeanne, also came to see Pasteur frequently.

On December 27, 1892, his seventieth birthday, Pasteur was honored with a grand jubilee celebration in the great amphitheater of the Sorbonne. Again, dignitaries and scientists from all over the world attended. As Pasteur shuffled slowly onto the stage on the arm of the president of France, the famous English physician Joseph Lister rushed up to greet him with open arms. Jean-Baptiste read Pasteur's brief remarks, in which he urged the young men in the audience, "Whatever your career may be, do not let yourselves be discouraged by the sadness of certain hours which pass over nations. Live in the serene peace of laboratories and libraries."[52]

British physician Joseph Lister (center) rushes to congratulate Pasteur (second from left) at the Sorbonne's 1892 grand jubilee celebration in Pasteur's honor.

Although he could no longer partici-pate in active research himself, Pasteur could take satisfaction in the work of his collab-orators as they began to make important discoveries through their research at the institute. In 1894, when Roux, working with Alexandre Yersin, developed a treat-ment for diphtheria, a common childhood disease that killed half of its victims, Pasteur rejoiced. Here was concrete evidence of what work done at the institute might mean to the welfare of all humankind.

The following year Pasteur spent much of his time sitting in the garden, watching the workers at the institute come and go. In this pleasant setting Marie and Marie-Louise read him memoirs of the Napoleonic Wars. On September 28, 1895, Louis Pasteur suffered a final stroke and died with Marie at his side holding his hand. The fiery patriot and tireless explorer was at rest, but his legend and his work would live on.

A Lasting Legacy

When Louis Pasteur died, he was treated as a national hero with every possible honor paid to him. By decree of the French government, his funeral was designated a national event and was paid for by the government. His body lay in state at the Pasteur Institute, where massive numbers of people filed by the casket. On October 5, 1895, thousands of people jammed the streets as the immense funeral procession, with full military escort, wound slowly through Paris from the Pasteur Institute to Notre Dame Cathedral for the official services.

The president of France, François Felix Faure, and his entire cabinet were in attendance, as were foreign leaders such as Grand Duke Constantine of Russia and Prince Nicolas of Greece. In a grand and solemn ceremony, tributes were paid to the man who had dedicated his life to science. Pasteur's final resting place was an ornate tomb built at the Pasteur Institute that was decorated in gold and marble with colorful mosaics depicting some of Pasteur's achievements. Marie Pasteur walked every day from her apartment at the institute down into the crypt to kneel next to her husband's tomb for a few moments. When she died in 1910, she was buried by his side, and their apartment was turned into a museum.

When the Pasteur Institute opened in 1888, Pasteur had said its mission would be "to deliver man from the calamities which beset him."[53] In the spirit and tradition of its founder, the Pasteur Institute has been responsible for many important discoveries. Over more than a century since it was founded, eight members of the institute's research staff have been awarded Nobel Prizes.

As Pasteur envisioned, the scientists at the institute have made great strides in preventive medicine developing vaccines for a number of contagious diseases. Other breakthroughs for the institute include the first drug to treat infections, the first antihistamine, and the identification of the human immunodeficiency virus (HIV). Outstanding scientists continue doing research there hoping to find cures for AIDS and cancer as well as vaccines for infectious diseases and allergies.

In 1900 Roux, the director of the institute, helped set up a teaching hospital in connection with the research institution. And the microbiology library of

This statue of Louis Pasteur stands at the Sorbonne in Paris. Pasteur's work eradicated many deadly diseases and laid the foundation for future research in preventive medicine.

one hundred thousand volumes is used by thousands of researchers each year. In addition, more than fifty branches of the Pasteur Institute have opened since 1888, including one in Saigon (now Ho Chi Minh City) Vietnam, in 1891 and one in New York in 1893.

The Pasteur legend continued to grow after his death. Villages, streets, and buildings were named after him. Statues and monuments, and pictures hung in classrooms and laboratories, remind students of the man who crusaded for the germ theory of disease. Not only did the germ theory revolutionize medicine, it affected the everyday life of ordinary people, who became aware of the importance of keeping their homes clean and of practicing good hygiene in handling food and taking care of their own bodies.

Some of the praise that was heaped on Pasteur shortly after his death painted him as a saint. A century later, some critics have gone to great lengths to try to discredit some of his work. The truth is that Pasteur was a complicated human being and therefore possessed human flaws, such as pride. What is undeniable is that he was a brilliant scientist. In an article in the *New York Review of Books,* Max Perutz, himself a distinguished biochemist, defended Pasteur against his critics, calling him "a good and just man who cannot defend himself because he is dead." Perutz did not deny that Pasteur had a large ego and loved recognition, but he said, "He was courageous, compassionate, and honest, and his scientific achievements, which have much reduced human suffering, make him one of the greatest benefactors of mankind."[54] A thoughtful consideration of Pasteur's life and work can hardly lead to any other conclusion.

Notes

Introduction: An Awesome Career

1. Quoted in David V. Cohn, "The Life and Times of Louis Pasteur," 1999, p. 2. www.labexplorer.com.
2. Quoted in René Vallery-Radot, *The Life of Pasteur*, trans. Mrs. R.L. Devonshire. Garden City, NY: Garden City Publishing, 1926, p. 444.

Chapter One: A Very Serious Young Person

3. Quoted in Louise E. Robbins, *Louis Pasteur and the Hidden World of Microbes*. Oxford, England: Oxford University Press, 2001, p. 16.
4. Quoted in Patrice Debré, *Louis Pasteur*, trans. Elborg Forster. Baltimore, MD: Johns Hopkins University Press, 1998, p. 16.
5. Quoted in Vallery-Radot, *The Life of Pasteur*, p. 15.
6. Quoted in Robbins, *Louis Pasteur and the Hidden World of Microbes*, p. 17.
7. Quoted in Vallery-Radot, *The Life of Pasteur*, p. 22.

Chapter Two: The Art of Crystallography

8. Quoted in Vallery-Radot, *The Life of Pasteur*, p. 23.
9. Quoted in Vallery-Radot, *The Life of Pasteur*, p. 32.
10. Quoted in Debré, *Louis Pasteur*, pp. 31–32.
11. Quoted in Gerald L. Geison, *The Private Science of Louis Pasteur*. Princeton, NJ: Princeton University Press, 1995, p. 60.
12. Quoted in René Dubos, *Louis Pasteur: Free Lance of Science*. New York: Da Capo Press, 1960, pp. 91–92.
13. Quoted in Dubos, *Louis Pasteur*, p. 95.
14. Quoted in Debré, *Louis Pasteur*, p. 48.
15. Quoted in Robbins, *Louis Pasteur and the Hidden World of Microbes*, p. 29.
16. Quoted in Debré, *Louis Pasteur*, p. 42.

Chapter Three: The World of the "Infinitely Small"

17. Quoted in Vallery-Radot, *The Life of Pasteur*, pp. 48–49.
18. Quoted in Vallery-Radot, *The Life of Pasteur*, p. 49.
19. Quoted in Debré, *Louis Pasteur*, p. 57.
20. Quoted in Debré, *Louis Pasteur*, p. 72.
21. Quoted in Dubos, *Louis Pasteur*, p. 18.
22. Quoted in Vallery-Radot, *The Life of Pasteur*, p. 79.
23. Quoted in Dubos, *Louis Pasteur*, p. 41.
24. Quoted in Debré, *Louis Pasteur*, p. 87.

Chapter Four: Not a Minute to Spare

25. Quoted in Debré, *Louis Pasteur*, p. 124.
26. Quoted in Vallery-Radot, *The Life of Pasteur*, p. 119.

27. Quoted in Robbins, *Louis Pasteur and the Hidden World of Microbes,* p. 45.
28. Quoted in Dubos, *Louis Pasteur,* p. 166.
29. Quoted in Debré, *Louis Pasteur,* p. 148.
30. Quoted in Geison, *The Private Science of Louis Pasteur,* p. 114.
31. Quoted in Dubos, *Louis Pasteur,* p. 177.

Chapter Five: Saving the Silk Industry

32. Quoted in Geison, *The Private Science of Louis Pasteur,* p. 31.
33. Quoted in Robbins, *Louis Pasteur and the Hidden World of Microbes,* p. 53.
34. Quoted in Vallery-Radot, *The Life of Pasteur,* p. 160.
35. Quoted in Vallery-Radot, *The Life of Pasteur,* p. 165.
36. Quoted in Vallery-Radot, *The Life of Pasteur,* p. 169.
37. Quoted in Debré, *Louis Pasteur,* p. 216.
38. Quoted in Debré, *Louis Pasteur,* p. 217.

Chapter Six: Battling Infectious Diseases

39. Quoted in Vallery-Radot, *The Life of Pasteur,* p. 184.
40. Quoted in Vallery-Radot, *The Life of Pasteur,* p. 291.
41. Quoted in Debré, *Louis Pasteur,* p. 278.

Chapter Seven: Creating Vaccines to Fight Disease

42. Quoted in Debré, *Louis Pasteur,* p. 318.
43. Quoted in Geison, *The Private Science of Louis Pasteur,* p. 46.
44. Quoted in Dubos, *Louis Pasteur,* p. 339.
45. Quoted in Robbins, *Louis Pasteur and the Hidden World of Microbes,* p. 81.

Chapter Eight: The Final Victory

46. Quoted in Vallery-Radot, *The Life of Pasteur,* pp. 360–61.
47. Quoted in Debré, *Louis Pasteur,* p. 438.
48. Quoted in Debré, *Louis Pasteur,* p. 440.
49. Quoted in Robbins, *Louis Pasteur and the Hidden World of Microbes,* p. 101.
50. Quoted in Robbins, *Louis Pasteur and the Hidden World of Microbes,* p. 102.
51. Quoted in Vallery-Radot, *The Life of Pasteur,* pp. 443–44.
52. Quoted in Dubos, *Louis Pasteur,* p. 56.

Epilogue: A Lasting Legacy

53. Quoted in Vallery-Radot, *The Life of Pasteur,* p. 444.
54. Max Perutz, "The Pioneer Defended," *New York Review of Books,* December 21, 1995.

For Further Reading

Books

Virginia Alvin and Robert Silverstein, *Rabies.* Springfield, NJ: Enslow, 1994. Reviews the history of rabies. Includes prevention and treatment and discusses current issues relating to the disease.

Beverley Birch, *Louis Pasteur: Father of Modern Medicine.* Woodbridge, CT: Blackbirch Press, 2001. Good color illustrations, timeline, and glossary of terms relating to microbiology.

Paul de Kruif, *Microbe Hunters.* New York: Pocket Books, 1940. Tells the story of great scientists (from Antonie van Leeuwenhoek to Paul Ehrlich) who pioneered in the world of diseases. Contains two chapters on Pasteur.

Sherwin B. Nuland, *The Doctors' Plague.* New York: W.W. Norton, 2003. Fascinating biography of the Hungarian obstetrician who (without the aid of a microscope) discovered the germ theory of disease decades before Pasteur, Lister, and Koch but failed to convince fellow physicians that germs were causing the high death rate of women during childbirth.

Greer Williams, *Virus Hunters.* New York: Knopf, 1959. Interesting profiles of men and women who worked on viral diseases in the nineteenth and twentieth centuries, including Edward Jenner, Jonas Salk, and Louis Pasteur.

Web Sites

American Library Association Science Experiments (www.ala.org). Major science website for young adults with over seven hundred links.

Pasteur Institute (www.pasteur.fr). Up-to-date information on the Pasteur Institute and its branches.

Video

The Story of Louis Pasteur, William Dieterle, dir. Warner Bros., 1936.

WORKS CONSULTED

Books

Patrice Debré, *Louis Pasteur.* Trans. Elborg Forster. Baltimore, MD: Johns Hopkins University Press, 1998. The author, a French physician, uses Pasteur's notebooks and writings to present a detailed account of Pasteur's life and scientific contributions.

René Dubos, *Louis Pasteur: Free Lance of Science.* New York: Da Capo Press, 1960. The author, a microbiologist, offers insights into the historical background that made Pasteur's discoveries possible.

Gerald L. Geison, *The Private Science of Louis Pasteur.* Princeton, NJ: Princeton University Press, 1995. This controversial biography by a history professor discusses ethical questions connected with Pasteur's scientific discoveries.

Louis Pasteur and Joseph Lister, *Germ Theory and Its Applications to Medicine* and *On the Antiseptic Principle of the Practice of Surgery.* Amherst, NY: Prometheus Books, 1996. In separate essays, Pasteur and Lister discuss the discoveries that led to the acceptance and application of the germ theory of disease in medical practice.

Louise E. Robbins, *Louis Pasteur and the Hidden World of Microbes.* Oxford, England: Oxford University Press, 2001. Examines the thought processes that led to Pasteur's discoveries and provides technical information to help understand them.

René Vallery-Radot, *The Life of Pasteur.* Trans. Mrs. R.L. Devonshire. Garden City, NY: Garden City Publishing, 1926. This biography by Pasteur's son-in-law provides intimate details of Pasteur's personality, family life, and relationships with contemporaries.

Periodical

M.F. Perutz, "The Pioneer Defended," *New York Review of Books,* December 21, 1995.

Internet Source

David V. Cohn, "The Life and Times of Louis Pasteur," 1999. www.labexplorer.com.

INDEX

Picture Credits

About the Author

Elizabeth Silverthorne lives in the village of Salado in the heart of Texas. She has studied writing at the University of Texas, Bread Loaf Writer's School in Vermont, and the Institute of San Miguel de Allende in Mexico. She taught English and children's literature at North Texas State University for four years and was director of communications and modern languages at Temple College for twelve years.

Silverthorne has written seventeen books for adults and children and numerous articles and short stories. Her specialties are history and biography, and she often travels extensively to research the places where her subjects lived.